W9-CYA-198

This book is dedicated to:

Joel, Jane , Alan and Debi

"Good ideas can happen on days of rest"

Note: Madrikhim are both boys and girls. For the sake of convenience the terms madrikh (a male leader) and madrikhim (many male leaders) will be used in odd-numbered chapters; madrikhah (a female leader) and madrikhot (many female leaders) will be used in even-numbered chapters.

TABLE OF CONTENTS

Foreward
The Curse of Joshua Mereminsky

In this introduction we are going to talk about the importance of being a madrikh or madrikhah. We are going to explain that it is actually part of a cosmic plan.

hen I was a kid, I used to think of myself as the worst terror who ever refused to take off his jacket during Hebrew School. I held the world's record for worst mutilation of a copy of *Ha-Yehudi Ha-Rishon*. I put chalk in every eraser and was the president of the drop-your-books-when-the-clock-strikes-4:51 club. Even so, I had a very calm, enlightened principal who used to respond to each of my escapades with a simple curse: "I hope someday, when you become a Jewish teacher, your students will treat you as well as you treat your teacher."

I would laugh. Each time she did it I laughed. I had absolutely no vision of myself as a Jewish teacher. It was last among all possibilities, somewhere just after street sweeping. Immediately upon my confirmation, Esther Starr Grossman, the principal, offered me a job as her office aide. These were the dark ages, long before teenagers were invited to work in classrooms. Mrs. Grossman also found me work as a Hebrew tutor. I was too flattered to say "No." Soon, with her help, I was working (as a high school student) towards my teacher certification at the Academy of Jewish

Studies. Once I was in college, Esther found me additional Hebrew tutoring work—and when I was ready to teach, but still too young to qualify for her elite faculty, she helped to find me my first teaching job.

Over the years, her curse has come true. I have learned repeatedly that I was far from a world-class disrupter of Hebrew School classes. My students have outclassed me. One of the greatest terrors I have ever taught was a small, hyperactive, brilliant imp by the name of Joshua Mereminsky. In a group, Joshua was just unteachable, but one-on-one I was taught much.

A couple of years ago, Joshua called and asked for advice. He was about to teach his first Hebrew School class. I immediately responded with the classic Jewish teacher's curse (taught to me so many years before): "May your students do to you—that which you did to me..."

Over the next several weeks, I spoke with many of Joshua's former teachers, now all rabbis and educators throughout the country, and shared with them my perception of Divine Justice. During that time, Joshua received a half-dozen phone calls from his former teachers, each welcoming him to the profession with a now-traditional folk curse.

Jewish teaching is a legacy. It is a mantle passed on from teacher to student. We have prepared this **Madrikhim Handbook** with one thought in mind: to give your Hebrew School teachers the last laugh.

Welcome aboard!

Joel Lurie Grishaver

Creative Chairperson, Torah Aura Productions

Using This Book

A NOTE TO BOTH ABOUT-TO-BE MADRIKHIM AND TO
ABOUT-TO-BE LEADERS OF MADRIKHIM PROGRAMS:

*In this introduction we are really explaining to
your teachers and principals the way to use this book.
We've included it here, because now that you are part
of the teaching team, you should be in on all the
planning.*

At present, there are many different kinds of
madrikhim programs all over North
America. They range widely in age requirements, intensity, responsibility, style, and
the kinds of pizza they order in for madrikhim meetings. In creating this **Madrikhim Handbook**, we have
tried to create a resource which will be valuable in a
majority of settings; that means that it will probably
meet the precise needs of no school. You will need to
make choices and adapt the chapters, exercises, discussions, and even commandments to your own
needs.

We've made the following assumptions:

**Madrikim work as teachers' assistants in class-
rooms.** While we know that some madrikhim work in
offices, some madrikhim serve as tutors, and that in a
few cases high school students even have their own
classrooms, we've centered this handbook on classroom support roles.

Madrikhim are part of a madrikhim program. We
assume that at least once a month madrikhim will

meet with a supervisor or master teacher and study the art of teaching. While the **Madrikhim Handbook** will perhaps be an even more valuable resource for madrikhim who aren't fortunate enough to be part of such a program, it was designed to facilitate this training. The other intriguing possibility that the **Handbook** enables, is the formal mentoring of madrikhim by their master teachers. Rather than being the basis for a class curriculum, the book can serve as a resource for a one-on-one tutorial.

Madrikhim are high school students. Yes, we do know that many eighth- and ninth-graders serve effectively as madrikhim, we know they do this with great maturity and skill. Even so, we've targeted this resource for tenth, eleventh, and twelfth graders. Younger, responsible, mature madrikhim will rise to the occasion.

Madrikhim should keep a journal. Our experience has suggested that one of the best ways to enter the field of Jewish education is through "reflective practice." The process of keeping a journal facilitates this reflection.

Imagining all the different ways this book will be used was lots of fun. Enjoy. If you ever invite me to one of your madrikhim meetings, my favorite pizza is mushrooms and olives.

B'Hatzlahah,
Rabbi Sam Joseph

For Your Journal

Inside this Handbook you will find directions for exercises designed to be written in your journals. You'll probably think of it as "homework." None of this "homework" is busywork or drill. It all has one of two purposes: either it will set you up to be ready for the next lesson or it will help you test out the things learned in the unit in the real world. This first assignment will set you up for the first lesson.

A Reflection on Being a Madrikh

1. Think of a teacher (or teachers) that you had in Jewish school whom you did not like at all. As you recall that class, list adjectives that describe that teacher. Once you have made your list, share it with other madrikhim.

2. Think of a teacher (or teachers) that you had in Jewish school whom you liked very much, whom you found special. As you recall that teacher(s), list adjectives that describe that teacher(s). Share this list with other madrikhim.

3. As you look at the two lists, how are you *not like* the teacher whom you could not stand? How are you *like* the teacher who was really special?

The Opening Credits
A Prologue to Chapter 1

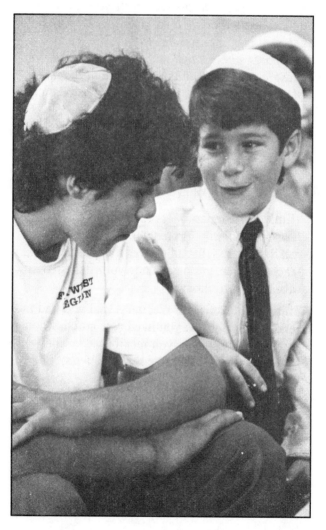

At the beginning of each chapter in this handbook you will find a page or more of material which we label a "prologue." Each of these prologues is a sketch of one or more real life experiences. They show you brief examples of the things which will be covered in the chapters. Later on, you'll learn that they are a kind of "set induction."

The day felt different—the day felt the same, (but we wouldn't go so far as to say that it was the best of days—the worst of days, etc.). This Sunday morning had started with mother telling Rob to button the shirt he wore over his t-shirt. He told her, "This is the way I always go to school." She said, "Today's different."

On the way into the building he slapped Jason a high-five and talked about the upcoming Thrasher championships. That felt the same. But, as the third-graders swarmed into Mrs. Levin's class, Rob was feeling nervous. He was a first-time madrikh. All of a sudden, that hit him in the pit of his stomach, sort of like a dull ache. It was almost the same feeling he had had the first time his parents had gone on a trip and left him by himself.

Less than a month ago, the educator at Temple Shalom had called and asked him to be one of the chosen madrikhim. Now, that seemed like years ago. Rob had gone to two meetings with his supervising teacher, Mrs. Levin. Together, the two of them did a lot of planning. Now it was all for real; the students were coming to class. Rob felt like a giant—he towered over these eight-year-olds.

Mrs. Levin greeted each of the boys and girls and motioned to Rob to join her. "Remember what we discussed Rob? You are part of this teaching team. Circulate around and make sure that the students are getting settled."

Rob scouted the room. Two students were standing bewildered by the chalkboard. Rob went over and said, "This could be a good place to sit. Try it out and I'll show you the stuff we're going to be doing. The two girls sat down and Rob brought them a copy of **Being Torah,** the book they would use this year.

"I think some of the photographs are really funny. Why don't you take a look and see of you can find the funniest one?"

"Thanks, teacher,"said one of the girls. Rob smiled both inside and out. This wasn't the same as being told to park his skateboard in the school office.

Chapter 1

ACTING LIKE A MADRIKH

Or Where Do I Stand?

In this first chapter, we are going to talk about the job of being a Madrikh. We'll explain the reason that madrikhim are really important to a school and discuss some of the difficulties of the job.

elcome to **Madrikh-hood**. We assume that if this handbook made it into your hands, a pretty good adventure awaits you. You are a high school student who is about to work in a Jewish school (or who is about to again work in a Jewish school) and the experience will be a challenge.

In some places the job goes by the name "teaching assistant," in others "teaching aide," and in others by the Hebrew term: *madrikh*, leader.

Madrikh (male) and *Madrikhah* (female) are two forms of the same Hebrew word which has been used for almost a hundred years for people who lead Jewish youth groups or work as Jewish camp counselors. In every case, a *madrikh* is somebody who helps Jewish learning happen in an informal way.

Don't worry—it will be a wonderful year. You will make countless errors. You will be excited, frustrated, challenged (and even sometimes bored) but you will get better in the process. And, believe it or not, you will make a major difference.

We suspect (from a lot of our own experience) that you will actually learn your job on your own. In truth, if anyone can be of help, it will be the classroom teacher(s) with whom you work and the person who supervises, guides and supports your activities. We already know that a book can offer only a little help, that of channeling your confusion in some given directions. We will give some hints and ask some questions, but ultimately, you (in dialogue with the others in the classroom) will define your own version of being a *madrikh*.

PRESTO: INSTANT MADRIKH

One of the difficult things about being a madrikh is that in one day you must move from being a student to being "one of the teachers." The last day of last year, you were one of the kids the teachers were trying to make learn. Now, just one school day later, you are being seen as a person with authority. Now, you are almost like a teacher, trying to see to it that your kids learn something. Suddenly, you have a whole new kind of responsibility.

A great rabbi, Abraham Joshua Heschel, who died just a few years ago, explained it this way, "What we need more than anything else is not more textbooks but textpeople. It is the personality of the teacher that the pupils read; the text they will never forget." You now have the responsibility to become that text!

YOUR JOB, SHOULD YOU CHOOSE TO ACCEPT IT...

The relationship between the people in a class-room is a contract. A contract is an agreement between two or more people which states the obligations of each involved party. In a classroom contract,
The teacher agrees:

to provide the structure,

to design and organize instruction,

to be responsible for being the source of authority,

to make the final decisions,

to shape and maintain an environment that makes it possible for the students to learn,

and to intervene when individual or class behavior is out of line.

The student agrees (joyfully or not):

to attend class,

to pay attention,

to make an honest effort to learn,

to behave appropriately

and to participate—

among other things.

But, as a madrikh, your responsibilities aren't as clear. What have you agreed to do? You are no longer a student—you are not yet a teacher. Yes, you are somewhere in between.

We know that the teacher stands at the front of the room and the students sit at their desks—your first job, then, is to figure out where the madrikh is positioned.

This course is designed to help you understand the terms of your "contract", and to guide you in finding your own way of fulfilling those promises. In a certain sense, it will tell you where to stand. To help, we will give you some practical advice, some theory, and some things to think about while you are in the classroom.

The actual responsibilities of each madrikh will vary from classroom to classroom, and school to school. Generally, however, your job is to assist the teacher, enhancing the students' experience in the classroom.

DUGMA IS DOGMA

One major part of your job has more to do with the way you *are* than with the specific things you *do*. It is called *Dugma Ishit*.

Dugma Ishit means PERSONAL EXAMPLE. It is the most crucial of all of your responsibilities. The students will be watching you closely to see how you act as their dugma. They will take their cues from your behavior and response to the rhythms of the class. Being a "dugma" means many things.

It means being a model of the right way to participate. When a teacher asks a group to sit on the floor and listen to a story, just by sitting among the kids on the floor and actively listening, you are helping by being a model of correct behavior. Sometimes, just by being an active member of the group (a ringer among the students) your presence can help to make an activity work.

As a madrikh, you are the example for the students in the school of how to act in a Jewish learning setting.

The students will look at you to see how they should respond in this learning setting.

In fact, this is also the way that you learn. There have been any number of people in your life who have acted as *dugmaot* for you. These individuals demonstrated by their words and actions how to live a Jewish life. Each of them in their own way left a little of themselves with you. Now it is your turn.

But, being a "dugma" also has a larger meaning. You are much closer in age to the students than the teacher, and so you are able to do something that the teacher cannot. Just by showing up weekly at the school (after you no longer have to) you show your students that Jewish education works. You are a living dugma. Your very presence makes a difference. If they see that you love being in a Jewish school, that you love being Jewish, it will have a terrific impact on them. We want every student who goes through the school to grow up to be like you—to think that school is so "cool" that if they are lucky (and good)—they, too, may ultimately get to work as a *madrikh*.

YOUR FUNCTION IN INSTRUCTION

Teaching is not one of your prime responsibilities. Most of the time you are there to *help* the teacher, not to *be* a second teacher. Although your teacher considers you a valuable partner—and it is possible that you may be given the opportunity to actually teach a particular lesson—your role is "support," although you may well teach one-on-one, tutor, or work with small groups.

So, what do we mean by "support" instruction?

Let's start with dugma. If nothing else has been specified, become an active student. As we have discussed before, just by "modeling" how a good student acts, you are helping the lesson work. ONE CAUTION: This does not mean answering questions! (Once in a while, the teacher may call on you for an answer, but by-and-large, raising the hand is a student job.) But it does mean singing loud, taking part in the dance, and maybe even working on your own version of a craft project. It also means not doing the wrong thing. Not talking while the teacher is, not refusing to dance, taking off your coat, and lots of other things help to establish the right way to act.

Particularly in the younger grades, students do a lot of individual work. Teachers often call these individual efforts "seat work." The students color, pour glitter, fill in worksheets, plan skits, etc. While this is happening, the teacher rotates around the room, visiting and encouraging individual students. This is an appropriate time for you to put on your "rock and roll shoes".

In older grades, there may well be a lot of group work. Small teams of students are asked to design a poster, plan a program, research a report, write a play, explain a passage, etc. In these cases, you may again move from group to group, or you may turn into a group leader, guiding your groups' work, a kind of super-student leader.

Support can also mean passing out the scissors, rewinding the tape, or figuring out how to program the VCR. If it will help the lesson to work, it is probably your job.

FEEDBACK

There is one place in the planning of instruction where you can be instrumental; that is providing feedback. The teacher has only two eyes, ears, hands, legs, and only one mouth. The teacher cannot be everywhere or see everything at once. You are able to observe and listen to one or two students while your teaching partner is doing something else. Evaluation of teaching methods is crucial to improving the learning process. You can help the teacher to evaluate the process by sharing your observations. How did Johnny respond to this filmstrip? Why does Shira seem so cranky?

You are an extra set of eyes, ears, hands, etc. and you have a whole other viewpoint. If your teacher is smart, she or he will (at the appropriate moments— and note the importance of timing) value your input in the planning and evaluation cycle.

ADMINISTRIVIA

The teacher is the one who must shape and maintain an **environment** that makes it possible for the students to learn. Creating such an environment involves a lot of logistics and paperwork. This is another area in which your support can make the difference between just another classroom and a place to which the students eagerly anticipate coming. A lot of being a madrikh is pouring juice and running to the office. This, too, makes a real difference.

Administrative support is a very important part of your job. By doing administrative stuff, you free the teacher to work with kids. The paperwork that begins each day is vital, not only to the school, but to your students. Attendance taking makes sense when you consider what happens if it doesn't happen. Collecting *tzedakah* does more than merely allow the teacher to work with the kids, it teaches and reteaches a vital lesson every class session.

Taking attendance is one of the ways a warm and loving teaching environment is created. It lets the students—and their parents, when they are called—know that someone cares very much whether or not the child is in class. It helps the members of the teaching team to be aware of who is and is not there at any given moment (very important when classes move to different rooms at various times during the day). It allows the teaching team to watch for trends—has little Rena missed every other week? That might indicate a problem at home of which the teaching team should be aware.

There are likely to be other functions you will perform that come under the category of creating a classroom environment—preparing bulletin boards and teaching materials, for example—and helping the teacher with them is a part of the reason you are in the classroom.

BEING THE HEAVY

Remember this: The teacher is the one responsible for intervening when individual or class behavior is out of line.

Let us learn two words. *Pro-active* and *Re-active*. Can you say "pro-active" and "re-active?" Proactive is an action you take before—it is prevention. Reactive is a response. The best classroom management is proactive, keeping students from ever getting out of hand. Most of your role in classroom management is proactive. You want to sit near problem kids, use your "evil eye" with great skill, master the gentle tap on the shoulder, and in other ways guide the classroom process from within.

As you establish a relationship with the students, your knowledge of each of them becomes a tool, making classroom management even easier. Once they like you (and they will—just because you have given up your free time to care about them), your opinion will make a difference to them. If they know that you disapprove of a certain behavior, they will think twice.

WARNING: your dugma can also have a negative impact. Do not be a negative role model; do not model behaviors we do not want imitated.

You, the madrikh, are a "textperson" for the students in your class. You will be the text that they will remember long after they have forgotten the textbook they used in the class.

CASE STUDIES:

Following is a series of case studies of different classroom and school situations. YOU are the madrikh. Decide what the problem is, what you would do and why you would do it. Discuss your answers with your fellow madrikhim and your supervisor.

Case #1

The whole upper school is in an assembly. You came in late and are sitting in the last row. Two kids who are not in your class (and whom you don't really know) are sitting just in front of you. They keep on talking. The principal has had to stop talking several times in order to wait for them to stop talking. They are disrupting the flow of the assembly, but nothing seems to stop them. Their teacher is way on the other side of the row and is not reacting. What should you do?

Case #2

You are standing around the hallway about fifteen minutes before class. Two of the kids in your class come up to talk to you. You are really pleased that they like you enough to want to talk to one of the "teachers" in the class. They tell you that they like you, but that the class is really boring and that the "real" teacher is mean. You, yourself, think that there are ways of making class more interesting—and that Ms. Hazaq is not exactly mean, but is certainly very strict. You want these kids to enjoy school—what should you do?

Case #3

It is the third or fourth week of school. You are working in a second-grade class. For the past two weeks you have noticed that Abe seems to have trouble with worksheets. Whenever they are passed out, he always colors over them rather than reading and filling out the questions. Usually, the teacher notices that Abe isn't working and sometimes encourages him to work. Other times, as long as he is quiet, he is left alone, even though the work isn't getting done. You always make a point of encouraging him. Sometimes, you'll read a question to him and he'll answer you, but when you leave him to write down the response, he's coloring again. What should you do?

COMMANDMENTS FOR MADRIKHIM

NEGATIVE COMMANDMENTS

1. Never model a behavior you do not want a student to copy. Do not talk during singing; do not eat before saying *ha-motzi*, etc.

2. Never contradict the teacher in front of the kids. You can question or object to anything—but do it later and in private.

3. Never get caught between the teacher and the kids. Telling the students, "I don't like this either, but I'm not the teacher…" doesn't help the process.

POSITIVE COMMANDMENTS

1. Be a positive dugma.

2. When nothing else is required of you, become an **active co-participant**; model the way a student should be acting.

3. Be **proactive**. Think about where in the room you could be sitting or standing to help with issues of "control" and "focus." Think about which student might need your help or attention. Think about what a teacher might need you to do next—what supplies are going to be needed?—what needs to be set up? etc.

Journal Entry

STALKING THE WILD SCHOOL CULTURE

This exercise is designed to get your thoughts ready for beginning the next chapter.

Stories are one of the best ways to uncover a culture. Knowing the stories people tell about a place is a good way of knowing its values and traditions. Pick three of these topics and write down a short (true) story about each.

Everyone knows that Mr/Miss/Ms./Mrs. _____ is the best teacher in the school...

One thing which happens every week is...

One program which everyone looks forward to is...

One special grade in this school is _____ because that year you get to....

One place in the synagogue which is special to most kids is...

The most important moment in the entire experience of someone going to this school is....

The worst moment in the entire experience of someone going to this school is....

The "wrong thing" most frequently done by students at this school is....

One "joke" or funny thing about this school which most graduates would share is....

How would you describe your school?

How would you describe the "successful" graduate of your school?

A RANDOM SAMPLE

A Prologue to Chapter 2

Thre are three synagogues in Sampleville, and while adults would try to explain the differences in terms of geography and ideology, the kids in Sampleville know the truth on a different level.

Adults will tell you that Temple Ramah serves the people on the hill. If you can't guess, the hill is the exclusive place to live. Use your imagination; you can already imagine what waits in the carpool lane. The school building is modern and well-stocked, and the teachers are well-paid. This is a place where everything is professional, and everything is "the best." More than 1800 children attend the school. There are more than 60 teachers on the faculty (and they don't even all know each other). The educational director and his three assistant principals run a tight ship. Everything is prepared and organized. This is a school which defines and follows the rules.

Ask the kids about Temple Ramah and they will tell you that Temple Ramah has a school uniform: Benetton. They also will tell you that this is a school where no one really knows you (unless you really want them to.) It runs like a very efficient factory. There are wonderful things to get involved with: plays, youth groups, family activities--if that is what you want. And a person can, if they want, slip by unnoticed and unchallenged. In that sense, Temple Ramah is an "easy" school for rich kids, but it has a lot of neat things you can do (if you are that type).

Adults start their description by saying that B'nai Horin is a synagogue which broke off of Temple Ramah. It is small, and also serves an affluent population, but is a place where families want to do things themselves. B'nai Horin has a lot of committees which meet a lot of times a year and actually make a lot of decisions. Their building is small, but highly artistic, and its walls are filled with art work created or purchased by congregants specifically for the synagogue. B'nai Horin is a creative place, where many of the congregants spend their time inventing and then re-inventing the way the congregation worships, acts with social responsibility, and makes decisions. (Yes, it is a place that has many meetings about how their meetings should work).

Kids call B'nai Horin a "funky" synagogue. When asked about the place, the school isn't the first thing they talk about. You hear stories about the building (and which part of it their parents helped to paint), the two weeks when everyone stopped everything to collect food to help those in an earthquake, the funny costume the rabbi wore on Purim, and when the synagogue president fell off the bima by mistake. When you ask about the school, the usual answer is, "It depends." When you ask for explanation, the answer is, "It depends on who you get." More questioning reveals that, by-and-large, parents run the school and teach in it—and even decide most of what and how they teach.

Beth Am is never called Beth Am, it is always called Rabbi Mercaz's shul. Adults will tell you that Beth Am is a medium-sized congregation located on the edge of the city, but close to the old suburbs where the majority of Jews used to live (the generation after the old Jewish neighborhood downtown).

This is the congregation that everyone's parents belonged to, and that now has a lot of third- and even fourth-generation families. It is a grand old building (now needing some renovation) with a wonderful feel of history. In a certain sense the worn marble steps feel comfortable. The one story you hear over and over is how Rabbi Mercaz knows everyone's name and everyone's life. He is notorious for congratulating people in the reception line on awards, promotions, and even good grades—things which no one thought he could possibly know about.

The kids at Beth Am also describe the synagogue in terms of Rabbi Mercaz. Each of them also has his or her own story about some special moments with the rabbi. Children who come from "active families" ("active" is their word) share some memorable moments spent learning or celebrating with the rabbi. Children who come from "not very religious families" ("religious" is their word) tell stories of being amazed that Rabbi Mercaz really knew them and was interested in them. When asked about the school, the usual answer is "Okay" Then they reel off a list of teachers and their skills (assuming that you and everyone else knows who they are—because it seems like all of them have been there forever).

Chapter 2

LIKE COUNTRIES, SCHOOLS HAVE CULTURE

Investigations into Uniqueness

This chapter focuses on the culture of your school. You already have some idea what a culture is: traditions, songs, customs, language, etc. In this chapter we will see how culture is important to a school and how understanding your school's culture is one key to your success as a madrikhah.

IS IT GOOD CULTURE OR CULTURE THAT TASTES GOOD?

I'll bet that you already know most or all of the three synagogues in Sampleville. They were easy to make up, because they came from pieces of synagogues you can find in almost every town. They come from elements common to the culture of many synagogues. In a certain sense, a synagogue is a living thing. It has a name, a way of doing things, things it likes, and things it hates. It has habits, customs, and even peculiarities which are often endearing. All of these elements are reflections of the "culture" of the synagogue community.

Jewish schools are part of synagogues. They share in the larger "culture" of the synagogue. Often, they also have a culture which belongs just to the school. Just as our symbolic Rabbi Mercaz could be so central to the lives of the congregants, many an educator, teacher, programmer, or youth leader is central to the lives of those who are part of his or her "sub-group." They may even be influential enough to affect the whole synagogue community.

Likewise, every classroom has its own culture which draws on the larger cultures of synagogue and school, but which is also very much shaped by the teacher and even you, the madrikhah.

THE IDEA OF A SCHOOL

Think about your family. Answer the question: "What makes your family a family?" You would probably start with the name and some pieces of family history. Then, you would talk about the things that your family does often. Then, finally, you would talk about the way your family does these things.

Think about it: How does your family pack the car for a vacation? I'll bet you have your own method or non-method. At the root of your family is a set of traditions and assumptions—and put together, these form a model, an idea of what your family is and how your family does things. There are Schwartz-like, Freedman-like, Rogolof-like, etc. ways of doing things.

Schools are like families. They are part ideology and part habit. Some things are done because they have been carefully thought through and some things are done because that is the way they have always been done.

The Jewish school in which you are now working—and every other kind of school as well—has an overriding philosophy that determines the ground rules for much of what is done there. While accidental or spontaneous moments may help to shape the way a school grows and evolves, a "good" school centers itself and organizes itself around a vision of what it means to be a "good" school.

Let us clarify with an example: Assume that the idea of reinforcing learning is a central part of the school's philosophy. One possible result might be a program for parents of Hebrew students, who could learn Hebrew in their own way to parallel what their kids are learning in class. That way, parents are able to talk with their kids about what they have all learned (and even help with homework). Through providing a parent Hebrew school program, the school is actualizing (making actual) its philosophy of reinforcement, providing many levels of support for the classroom experience.

Other aspects of school life may be instinctive and not completely thought through. In one school we know well, the principal, Joyce, makes it a practice to stand at the top of the steps during the fifteen minutes when kids come into the building. She talks to each kid and knows each of them well enough to know the right question to ask to really show them her interest. She does it because she likes to do it, and because she has a feeling that this is the "right way" to run a school. When you walk around the school, you see most of the teachers doing the same thing. Pre-class is a time when teachers and madrikhim work hard to get to really know their students. This didn't start out to be a formal part of the school philosophy, rather it grew organically as part of the school culture. It started just because Joyce liked doing it. Eventually, Joyce and her staff realized the impact this informal welcoming had, and have formally made it part of the school's philosophy. Now, when new staff are brought onto the faculty, both the practice of welcoming students and the reasons for doing so are part of the training.

Details of the daily running of the school and the routines of the staff are important in telling about the values and attitudes of the school. These habits and practices tell a lot about the true values of the school culture. The curriculum of the school should also be a reflection of what the community deems important for a synagogue member to know and do as an adult. We know of one school whose formal philosophy, the one published and sent to parents, quoted a major scholar in their movement that they will teach "Hebrew as the living vernacular of the Jewish people." That is, Hebrew as a way that Jews communicate. Yet, when you examine their Hebrew program, you will find that it centers almost exclusively on the oral reading of the prayerbook. When the contradiction was pointed out to the congregational educator, the response was immediate—next year we'll edit the quotation. Often, to discover what a school really believes, you must look not only at what it says, but also at what it does.

Be True To Your School

Philosophy is a word that describes ideas. For ideas to have an effect, someone has to believe in them, and then put them into action. The process of putting the school philosophy into action creates a culture. Sometimes, schools base their philosophy on ideas (such as those worked out by scholars). Other times, philosophies grow out of intuitive feelings or important experiences. Schools are always evolving and changing, and this means their culture, too, is also always changing.

Each and every school has a culture. Knowing what makes up this culture, and being able to describe it, will help you to understand your own role as a madrikhah. You will see that the culture of your school ultimately defines what is success in your school.

THE WELL-CULTURED MADRIKHAH

By now, you have probably asked yourself: "Self, what does all this talk of culture have to do with pouring juice and collecting pencils?" The answer: Your job is more than that.

Let's talk about carnivals, the kind you may have visited, but more probably, the kind you've only seen at movies. This kind of carnival is the kind with side shows and games. Each exhibit has to draw people in. Each exhibit has to get people to buy into its experience. Carnivals do this with two kinds of employees, though most people only know about one of them. They are "barkers" and "shills." The barker stands out in front and gives the "spiel." This is the "patter" which tells people about all the exciting things they can experience or win. (Yes, "spiel," which became carnival slang, is really a Yiddish word. It is the play we perform on Purim.) At the end of the "spiel," the barker wants someone to be first, to be the first one to play the game, or to be the first one to pay the money to go in to see the show. This first customer "breaks the ice" and gets the crowd moving. It works even better if the first customer wins something, or talks loudly about how excited he or she is. After awhile, carnivals figured out that they were better off providing their own first customers who could perfectly "break the ice." To insure success, they created a job called "shill." The shill is a professional perfect first customer.

Jewish schools have learned the same lesson. We use a different name. We call our own perfect first customers madrikhot. The "barker" and the teacher, the "shill" and the madrikhah, share a culture. (Yes, "shilling" is another way of being a dugma.)

Madrikhot also have an important second role. Your job is also to be the one who can "fill in," the person who picks up the almost dropped piece, the one who shoves a quick piece of chewing gum into the cracks. You are the tinkerer, the fixer of small but important details. Knowing the philosophy and understanding the culture of your school must be at the center of your work. That knowledge and those understandings are what will empower you, and give you the freedom to improvise. By knowing all of the ground rules—both written and unwritten—you can constantly find and redefine your place as a madrikhah within the classroom and the school. Let's face it, there will be times when in the thick of instruction, (with Chad almost crying, Roger shooting paper clips, Cindy and Felise bouncing off the walls, the music specialist out sick, and the photocopy machine not working) when no one is going to have the time to tell you exactly what to do. When you really understand your school, you won't need those instructions, you won't need to ask, and you won't even need to think about it—you will just know.

Becoming a madrikhah is a lot like learning to drive. You have to spend a lot of time focusing, analyzing, and thinking about behaviors which work well only when they become reflexes.

CASE STUDIES

Please read these case studies. Discuss them with your fellow madrikhot.

Ask yourself: "How does our school deal with this kind of situation? What is our way of rewarding, structuring, disciplining, etc? How would the rabbi, the principal, the best teacher, etc. deal with this situation? What is "our" way?

Case 1

Ben is a classic pain. He often gets out of hand. He has the kind of energy which makes you think that seatbelts on the desks ought to be a federal regulation. His problem can be defined in two words: "self" and "control." When Ben wants things, he wants them now. He is not hateful, or evil. Causing trouble or hurting other people is not something he wants to do—he just needs his needs fulfilled now, and now, and now, and now!

Today is no exception. During the first half hour Ben has disrupted the class 22 times (a new personal best). Finally, it is obviously time for action when he tries to finger paint with another student's fingers across the back of a third student's sweater.

What is our way of dealing with Ben? What is our way of doing what is best for both Ben and the class? In what way can you as madrikhah, the first one to deal with Ben on this issue, begin our way of handling this situation?

Case 2

Rachel is great. She is a seventh-grade student who is always prepared. She is also your sister's best friend.

You know that she is really involved in the lesson each week. Amazingly for seventh grade, she can even pull off the trick of motivating her classmates with her enthusiasm. You think that in three years she will be the perfect madrikhah.

You hear from your sister, however, that she is planning to drop out of Religious School after her Bat Mitzvah. Even though she likes being at the synagogue, her private school is very demanding and so are her dance lessons. She says, "As much as I hate it, I have to make choices. That's becoming an adult."

What is our way of dealing with Rachel? What will we do about it? Who will be the person(s) to act? Will the knowledge that I have be useful? To whom? In what way can you as madrikhah, the first one to deal with Rachel on this issue, begin our way of handling this situation?

Case 3

Jon is a regular second-grader. He usually enters the room with a big smile and a lot of noise. Today he was quiet.

When you ask him, "Why are you so quiet today?" he tells you, "My grandma is old and has been real sick this week."

Later that morning the people in the office get a call from Jon's mother. She says that his grandma has died and that she is coming to get Jon.

How will our school deal with Jon and his family that day? What kind of follow-up will our school/community do? What part in these responses should or could you (as madrikhah) play?

Case 4

The Rabbi announces that the congregation is going to get a new Torah Scroll. The Sofer is going to finish the last few lines at the synagogue as part of a special service of dedication.

The congregation wants to make sure that the Religious School and the Hebrew School are to be involved in the acquisition. They want every student to feel very much a part of this unique time in the life of the congregation.

What is our way of involving the school in the life of the congregation? How will we make this involvement happen? What part of this process can a madrikhah perform?

COMMANDMENTS FOR MADRIKHOT

Negative Commandments

1. Never talk of the school as "they" or "you." The school is always "we." Never think that you are outside of the school culture. Your students and their families think of you as part of the school—no matter what you say or do.

2. Never think that you are powerless, that you cannot have any influence on what the school is. As part of the teaching team and a member of the school community, you can be a strong influence on that which your school is constantly becoming. Remember, for many of your students and their families, you are a large part of their experience of the school.

3. Never think that you will be done learning how our school works. Our school is constantly growing and changing. You will always have more to learn.

Positive Commandments

1. Always be a representative of the school culture, a representative of the school. It is highly likely that you will see your students at parks, pizza parlors, and performances of **Phantom of the Opera**. How you say, "Hello," how you react to them there, is also part of their relationship with the school.

    Think about the complicated message when you run into a school family at a Friday night movie when neither of you are at services. What could be positive about that experience?

2. Be an active part of the congregation as well. Joining as an active part of holiday celebrations, social action (*tikkun olam*) events, and even fundraisers can be an important part of the dugma you present. It is another way of saying that which we are teaching is important enough for me to live.

3. Always believe that each and every thing you do as a madrikhah is important. That is the way culture works.

Journal Entry

RESEARCH ON SCHOOL CULTURE

Sit with your supervising teacher (the one with whom you will work as a madrikhah and conduct an interview. Explain to the teacher that you are attempting to learn about the customs and traditions of our school. If your supervising teacher is new to the school, arrange to interview someone who is more of a veteran of the school.

a. What are the really special whole-school events in the school year?

b. What are the really special events that take place for our grade, or that take place for students in our classroom?

c. What is an important "ritual" in our school?

d. What is unique about this school? What special ways of doing things does it have? What makes it different from the other Jewish schools in this area?

e. How does this school define an "excellent student?" In what ways do we show students and teachers what we mean by "excellent?"

f. Does the school (or congregation) have a logo or a motto? What does it say about the school?

THE DITTOS FROM BEYOND TIME

A Prologue to Chapter 3

No one knows the true origins of the Passover holiday dittos. They have been around the school forever. They have been runoff year after year, traced and retraced, and now, in the past two generations, they have made the transition from spiritmaster (ask someone to explain—spirit masters are a piece of education history) to photocopy, and now they have been scanned and desktop republished on the school computer.

The Passover holiday dittos are six pages. Each page has a big picture of some Passover symbol to color and underneath it there is some kind of fun activity like a crossword puzzle, a rebus (one of those stories where you have pictures stuck in the middle of sentences and you have to figure out what word they stand for), and the like. Every kid at Anshe Example Benevolent Synagogue (a.k.a "The Temple") knows them well. Every year, the week before the model Seder, there are piles of them in the school office; teachers are free to take and use them (as they feel the need).

In kindergarten, there are eleven minutes of excitement when the Passover dittos are passed out. Crayons fly both across the pages and across the room. A few of the crayon marks fall within the lines, most of them form great blotches of color. The creative exercises at the beginning are left untouched, except for the occasional ricochet of a crayon off a drawing, or the splotch of some post-modern placement of a balancing color area. A good time is had by all, except for Jennifer who is mad because all her crayons were broken and Jeremy got whole ones.

In first grade, the students begin coloring the Passover dittos even before the teacher can explain what to do. The sweet smell of cherry and grape felt-tip markers fill the room. The teacher does a little bit of question-asking and discussion. Some kids participate and some continue coloring, except for Chad who is playing with some of the Montessori toys which are in the room (even though they belong to the pre-school which rents the building during the week). In the middle of talking to the class, the teacher feels a tug on her dress. She bends down and Shana whispers in her ear, "We did this last year." She turns and whispers back, "I know, but this year we're going to do something different with it." Shana whispers back, "Okay" After a few more minutes' coloring, the teacher asks the class, "Who wants to read the bottom of the first page?" Lots of hands go up. One by one the students are called upon to read. A few of the words are difficult, but the teacher helps them sound them out. The rebus is far too difficult for them to figure out on their own, but the teacher walks them through it. When the class begins to lose focus, they are quickly directed to a new activity. The class moves to the story circle and Craig, the madrikh, cleans up the table. A good time is had by all, except for Craig who is left looking for the covers to one grape- and two lemon-flavored felt-tipped markers.

In second grade, there are only pencils; there are no crayons and no markers. The teacher introduces the exercises at the bottom of the ditto-pages as a contest: the boys' table against the girls' table. The first table to finish all six work sheets—correctly (the teacher emphasizes)—is to be the winner. The action is fast and furious. It takes about nine minutes to do, thirty minutes to go over, and one five-minute water and bathroom break, to finish the entire lesson. A good time is had by all, but especially Dawn and Rachel, the madrikhot who were the "captains" of the two tables.

The third- fourth- and fifth-grade teachers decide not to use the famous Passover dittos. They have developed other resources. For the most part, their kids, too, have a good time.

The sixth-grade teacher saw the Passover dittos in the office, and even though they weren't part of his lesson plan, he decided to use them as a review. When class begins, he asks a few review questions about Passover. No one has any answers to give. The room is dead silent until Jason "accidentally" knocks all his books off his desk with a "thud," and Matt does the same thing. Over the next fifteen minutes, the class uses pencils and pretends to complete the worksheets. They are turned into original art projects (punk and heavy metal modifications are common) and airplanes, and Steven and Faj turn one into a football for that game where you flick field goals between the other player's thumbs. In this lesson, a good time is had by everyone but the teacher.

Elana and Debi are in ninth grade. On their way into Wednesday night class, they stopped in the office to say hello to the school educator and tell her about the Arab-Israeli argument they had in their political science class. They see the piles of the Passover dittos and decide to bring them into class. They tell everyone, "Look what we found." The class spends a few minutes reminiscing about how many times they had filled them out, and about what happened in each class. Ira slips into the second-grade classroom and borrows the crayon can. When the teacher walks into class, his ninth-graders are busy coloring, talking, reviewing, and enjoying the Passover dittos.

Dr. Faust got to adult education early. He took his cup of coffee into the room. He found a leftover copy of the dittos on one of the desks. He began to fill it out. When Mrs. Hoffman came in, he asked her if she thought that "Afikoman" was the right answer to four across. One by one the whole class was involved in trying to figure out the answers. When the rabbi saw what was happening, she ran to the office and got a set for everyone. They spent twenty minutes using it as a foundation for their own review, before they got back to talking about the philosophy of Mordechai Kaplan.

At the end of the class, Mrs. Freed asked if she could have an extra set to send to her grandchildren. Two weeks later, she told the rabbi her daughter had said that the whole family had a good time going over these worksheets, two of which were still on their refrigerator door.

Chapter 3

GROWING UP
Studies in Child Development

This is the scientific chapter. It talks about the way children grow and what they are capable of doing at each stage. This is important knowledge for any teacher or any madrikh because it lets us set and test our expectations.

Every time you enter a classroom you will be working with a group of children, each of whom is very unique (and if it is a Jewish school, all of whom are above average). There is no way that a book can tell you how to relate to each of them. However, it is possible to give you some insights; child development is one key.

The term "development" (in its most general educational sense) refers to changes that occur in human beings; the growth which stretches from birth to death. Generally development is divided up into various aspects: physical development, changes in the body; personal development, changes in personality; cognitive development, changes in the way a person thinks; and social development, changes in the way a person relates to others.

How a person's thinking and reasoning ability develops is an area of special interest to educators. It is vital for teachers to be aware of how a child develops. With a solid knowledge of what students at a certain age level can do, think about or know, what their social grouping is like, how they make decisions, how they organize their world, the teacher can plan and create lessons that are going to be meaningful for that specific age level. Good teaching must learn a lesson from Goldilocks and the Three Bears; good teaching is not too hard, not too easy—good teaching is just right.

It is equally important for you, the madrikh, to have an understanding of the phases of development that a child undergoes. While it is the teacher's job to gear the presentation to fit within the framework of the class's ability to understand, you too will need to understand the capabilities of your students.

THE CHILD INSIDE THE PERSON

The very next sentence will teach you the essence of this entire chapter: **Remember what it was like to be 6 years old; to be 10 years old; to be 12 years old?** If you can get in touch with the part of yourself that is the same age as the kids in your class, you will be able to understand much of what they are understanding and respond to them in a manner that will reach them—to which they will respond.

Try this: Imagine that you are sitting next to little Yosi. The teacher has just explained, "A kiddush cup is a way we recognize the holiness of a day?" Yosi whispers to you "I don't understand. What is a kiddush cup?"

How would you explain it to Yosi? Would you explain the same way to a six-year-old as you would to a thirteen-year-old or to a sixteen-year-old? At which age would you use pictures? At which age would you use an example from their own life? At which age would you compare the concept of a kiddush cup to the pouring of libations in ancient Greece? You, of course, might have an even better way to explain the kiddush cup to a child of each age, but you would have to explain it differently to each, depending on their ages.

YOU NEED THE RIGHT TOOLS FOR THE JOB

Jean Piaget (Pea-ah-zhay), a Swiss psychologist, offers us some help in locating the child inside. He was a great observer of children and he developed a theory of how children grow in the area of cognitive development—how they learn to think. Piaget literally spent years watching and listening to children.

Piaget teaches that there are actually ways of thinking which are quite simple and natural for adults, but which are impossible for young children (no matter how smart). This would mean that a teacher must limit the material to be presented to the student, not only in terms of the amount, or the complexity, or the speed, but also in terms of the *kinds* of reasoning involved.

Piaget divided cognitive development into four stages.

Sensorimotor	ages 0-2 years
Pre-operational	ages 2-7 years
Concrete Operations	ages 7-11 years
Formal Operations	ages 11-15 years

Please note that the ages given are approximations and may vary from child to child.

PRE-OPERATIONAL

From two to seven, children really begin to develop language skills. They quickly get better and better at expressing themselves with words, at reading, and finally at writing. They have very vivid imaginations. They can be easily involved in and easily frightened by their fantasies. For the child at the pre-operational level, the line between reality and fantasy may be unclear. This child has difficulty seeing things from another person's point of view. For the child at this stage, the entire world revolves around him or her, and he or she expects that teachers and fellow classmates will act only in response to his or her needs.

The single most important word in the two-year-old's vocabulary is "MINE!" It takes a long time for children to say, "WE!" Even though *sharing* and *co-operation* are a big part of playgroups, preschools, kindergartens, and primary school, most kindergarten and first-grade classes are made up of 15-30 children, each of whom is psychologically "the only student in the room." This is part of the challenge.

Hints For Working With The Pre-operational Level

1. Use concrete props and visual aids. Show pictures, physically demonstrate what you are talking about, show objects.

2. Make instructions and directions relatively short, using actions as well as words. You do

not want the students to get confused. Show
them how to do the project. Explain the game
by acting out the part of a participant.

3. Do not expect the students to see the world
from someone else's point of view. Avoid long
lectures about worlds too far away from the students' experience. Avoid long lectures.

4. Emphasize physical activities. Whenever possible an idea should be connected to an action.
Give students a great deal of physical practice
with things. Have them hold the siddur, kiddush cup, put on a kipah.

5. Plan for short attention spans. The secret to
the younger grades is to teach an idea through
three, four, or five different five-to-ten-minute
activities rather than through one long half-
hour event.

CONCRETE OPERATIONAL

Between the seventh and eleventh year children
become more and more able to solve problems by
logic. They can understand that Shabbat Candles are
lit first and then blessed, because if you blessed them
first you would be kindling a flame on Shabbat (and
breaking a Shabbat rule). If you ask them "What do sitting at the table on the first night of Passover, the first
night of Rosh Ha-shanah and on Shabbat have in common?" they could answer, "On all of them we light
candles, say *Kiddush*, and make a *motzi* over bread."

Children at this level of development still have a difficult time with hypotheses—"what-if" questions—but

they are good at thinking about actual things. That's why we call it "concrete."

Children between seven and eleven like to classify things. This is sometimes carried to an extreme. Things are put into rigid categories—people are good or bad, friend or enemy. Everything is black or white: they see no gray. They learn the rules to games and are very much interested in everyone obeying the rules. These rules help them practice the logical thinking that they can now do.

This is the age of collections, baseball cards are sorted and ordered, Barbie doll wardrobes are carefully assembled. Children of this age live in a wonderful chaos which has some carefully ordered areas.

Hints For Working With The Concrete Operational Level

1. Continue to use concrete props and visual aids, but in using them, focus on grouping, sorting and organizing. If you must deal with history (an abstract idea) use time lines to help make comparisons concrete.

2. Make sure that lectures and readings are brief and well organized. Materials should move step by step. Stories should be short and to the point. Attention spans have increased, but they are still not even teen-age length, let alone adult.

3. Do not ask the students to deal with more than three or four variables at a time. Readings should have a limited number of characters. Projects need to have a limited number of

steps. The process of correlating two or more elements (like graphing) is an abstract skill which will be very difficult, if not impossible, for them.

4. Use familiar examples to help explain more complex ideas so that students will have a beginning point for understanding the new information. Compare the students' own lives with the story you are reading. Use stories whenever possible.

FORMAL OPERATIONS

Between ages eleven and fifteen most children develop the ability to think abstractly. Students at this level can be given a problem and they will solve it logically and systematically. They can handle a problem such as, "If we tell the story of the person who needs the money we can collect more *tzedakah*, but if we tell the story we will embarrass the recipient." What should be done? These children are capable of considering many alternatives at once, and this can mean that they sometimes get carried away with an activity. They can spend hours working on all the details they can find and lose sight of the original project.

Hints for Working With Students Beginning Formal Operations

1. Use many teaching strategies and materials. Now, charts , graphs and other more sophisticated pieces can be presented.

2. Give students opportunities to explore hypothetical questions. Questions about social issues, "what-if's", and things without easy answers are much more challenging to them.

3. Encourage students to explain how they solve problems. Ask them to do more than just repeat one final answer. Have them justify their answer.

It was not that many years ago that people looked at children and saw them as small adults. The child was viewed as an empty container to which different amounts and kinds of substances would be added until the container was full and the child emerged as an adult.

We know that the child is not just one, but many separate containers, each a different size and shape depending on the child's stage of development. The difference between a child and an adult is not just the quantity of "knowledge" that the two possess, but also the quality of that "knowledge". Children have less knowledge than adults in particular areas **and** they have different ways of knowing. The more we can look into their world, the easier it is to communicate.

BE A ZONE TROOPER

Meet the letters ZPD; they hold a secret. ZPD stands for the Zone of Proximal Development. The ZPD is the secret which lets Piaget really help you be a madrikh or a teacher. A lot of research has shown that when a child is growing from one stage into another, it is possible to encourage that development by helping and modeling. A student who can't do a task alone, may be able to do it first with some help, and then repeat it alone. Think about it—I bet you can remember an example. If the student is in the ZPD for a particular skill or insight, you can provide the "scaffolding" which will help them make the transition.

As a madrikh it will be important for you to be an astute observer of the children in your class. You will want to be aware of where they are starting at the beginning of the year...starting in the sense of what they know and what they can do....and to constantly work with them as they grow during the year. By watching, remembering, and understanding, you can actually help them grow.

CASE STUDIES

Read each of the following case studies and determine:

at what age/grade the activity is too juvenile.
at what age/grade the activity is age appropriate.
at what age/grade the activity is too difficult.
how the activity can be adapted to the grade you work with.

1. The teacher asks the class to tell him how the Shabbat is a taste of the time of the messiah.

2. The class takes a field trip to the cemetery, learning about the lives of the people buried there from a member of the congregation, making pencil rubbings of the beautiful engravings, and learning that while death may bring sadness, it is not an evil thing.

3. To learn about Jewish history.and archaeology, a "tel"—or mound—is made in the synagogue parking lot by having a truckload of sand poured there. Before class each week, the madrikhim plant "artifacts" in the mound for the students to dig up with teaspoons, which they bring back to class and discuss.

4. The teacher lectures the class about ten different Jewish ideas about God.

5. The class has to write a story entitled,"What if I could make everyone in the world ....?"

6. The members of the class are each given roles and asked to re-enact the Nuremberg War Crimes Trials.

7. The class builds a model of the Temple in Jerusalem during the time of Solomon out of modeling clay.

8. The teacher asks the students to draw a picture of wind. The class then compares trying to draw "wind" to trying to draw "God."

9. The class watches a video about Miriam Mendelow and *Yad L'Kashish* (Lifeline for the Old in Jerusalem) and talks about what old people are and are not capable of doing.

10. The class plans a career day to learn about working in the Jewish community. They have the teacher ask several speakers to come to their class to describe the work that they do.

COMMANDMENTS FOR MADRIKHIM

NEGATIVE COMMANDMENTS

1. Don't expect a six-year-old to act like a sixteen-year-old, and don't expect a sixteen-year-old to behave like a six-year-old.

2. Don't treat Piaget's levels as if they were laws engraved in stone. A student is allowed to act older or younger than Piaget says they should. His levels are only a guideline for you.

3. Don't ask a student to do something that you would not be willing to yourself—now, or especially when you were their age.

POSITIVE COMMANDMENTS

1. Try to remember what it was like to be six or ten or whatever age your students are.

2. Make sure that students have opportunities to set and work towards realistic goals. Have many short projects that offer true gains.

3. Let students show their independence and responsibility. Tolerate or even encourage noble mistakes. Encourage initiative and growthful risk-taking in the classroom.

Journal Entry

DO IT YOURSELF

You can test how students at different age levels think by asking them some questions. Try asking these same questions to students of various ages and compare their answers:

What does it mean to be alive?
Can you name some things that are alive?
When is yesterday?
Where do dreams come from?
Where do they go?
Why are people good?
How do you know when you have hurt someone?
What is beauty?
In what ways are you like God?

RESEARCH

You will need to arrange opportunities for yourself to visit and observe three different age levels of classes in your school. The purpose of these observations is for you to look at and closely observe how different age levels work, think, learn. By observing three levels you will be able to compare and contrast the developmental changes between the different levels.

Arrange to spend at least one-half hour in a Kindergarten or first-grade class; one-half hour in a third- to fifth-grade class; one-half hour in a seventh- to ninth-grade class. In each class you will need to take notes on the following questions:

1. How well do the students read and write? (Do they write or "letter"?)
2. Do the students freely mix with classmates of the opposite sex?
3. What kinds of activities does the teacher use during the class period?
4. How does the teacher use physical activity during class?
5. How often does the teacher change activities? (every 5 minutes, 10 minutes, more, less?)
6. How do students think about topics in terms of themselves, in terms of rules, in terms of ideas? etc.
7. Are students encouraged to explain how they arrived at an answer? When the teacher asks "Why do you say that?" how do they answer?
8. If the class is doing an art project, or there is completed art work in the room, what do you notice about the work? How neatly is it done? How precise is it?

Gather your notes from each of the observations and combine them for an overall view of the three different levels you observed. Compare your findings with the other madrikhim, and with Piaget's levels.

Journal Entry

This "homework" assignment is designed to provide you with some insights which will help you in the next unit. Believe it or not, before writing this journal entry, we want you to watch television.

To understand how lessons are put together, you are going to watch one of the most effective teachers of all time, your television set. You are going to pick a half-hour or hour comedy or drama and observe the techniques it uses to draw you in and keep you from changing the channel. You are also going to observe the way it teaches you.

1. Pick out the program of your choice. Look it up in the TV guide. Watch for commercials about the program. In what ways does a television network prepare you to watch a show?

2. Start watching the channel at least fifteen minutes before the program is scheduled to begin. Make note of everything done to direct your attention to the program.

3. From the first seconds of the teaser (the first part of the program shown to you) through the final tag (the part of the program after the program) make a list of:

   a. everything which is done to attract your attention and set your expectations.
   b. everything which is done to keep you from drifting away.

c. every piece of information (important to the show) which is presented.

4. Afterwards, prepare notes for an essay (which we will not make you write) entitled: "What can we learn from the way television motivates and teaches?"

GETTING SET

A Prologue to Chapter Four

This chapter will talk about the planning and structuring of lessons. It will deal with the beginning, middle, and end of each lesson. It has a prologue, an intermission, and an epilogue. These will match up with our discussions of the beginning, middle, and end.

Franci Goldberg's Three-Ring Kindergarten: Act One

The room was set up in advance. On the table were parts of costumes: two crowns (from a fast food restaurant), a three cornered hat (left over from a trip to historical sites in Boston), a big ring, an old baton covered in aluminum foil to serve as a sceptre, a druze hat, and a home made harem hat made from an old see-through scarf. Hanging on the board, ready to unroll, was a giant scroll. As the kindergarten students entered the room, each one was carrying a noise-maker. There were airhorns and homemade rattles, pots to bang with a wooden spoon, and Crystal brought a cymbal that you work with your foot. It came from her brother's drum set. As the kids came in, Franci and her two madrikhim fussed over each and every noisemaker.

When she was ready to begin, Franci pulled a big wooden gragger out of her pocket book. She swung it and made lots of noise. She surprised herself at how loud it was. She laughed and then swung it some more. The room got quiet. Franci said softly, "Circle time." Everyone dove for a good spot on the carpet. The madrikhim scanned the array of kids, then each chose the right place to set up their zone defense.

Franci ran the opening ceremony. Each kid picked up his or her Polaroid™ photograph and told one good thing which had happened during the week. Franci and the madrikhim worked hard, keeping the noise-makers out of use. When attendance and the circle ritual were finished, Franci gave another big crank on her gragger and then shouted, "Let's see how much noise we can make!" The whole room banged and tooted and shook. Then she shouted "Stop!" She took out a white flag. She said, "Whenever I raise my white flag, everyone has to stop." The class practiced making noise and then stopping twice.

Franci then asked, "What story are we going to become today?" The whole class shouted, "Esther." "I want you to raise your hands if you want to answer this question. Who are the people in the Esther story?" The kids raised their hands and named, "The King," "Esther," "Haman," "Mordechai," and the others. Franci thought to herself, "It really does make a difference if the parents read the story to their own kids before they come to class. Sending the booklets and the letter home really did make a difference." "Okay, she said, "Let's put on a show!" She picked up the King's crown and got ready to cast the story..."

Jane Ellen's Fourth-Grade Academy: Act One

When students come into Jane's fourth-grade room, they know that it is their responsibility to "be prepared" to learn. In her first few lessons of the year, Jane drills into her students that "prepared" is "pre-pared" and that means "you get pared **before** I'm ready to teach." Being prepared means (1) checking off your own name on the attendance chart, (2) taking your own copy of **Being Torah** out of the bookshelf in the back of the room, and (3) having a "writing implement" and something to write on.

While the class is getting ready, Jane is busy arranging her things and making sure that Scott, her madrikh, knows what will be happening.

Jane begins the lesson by picking up a large magnifying glass which is on her desk. She walks around the room carefully examining things: Debora's hair, Kent's doodles on the bookcover he made for his **Being Torah**, and Zipper's eyelashes. (Yes, Zipper's name is really Zipper—his mother said, "It's a long story" and she's never told it to Jane).

In a couple of quick teacher questions (officially called a socratic dialogue) Jane and the class establish that a magnifying glass lets you examine something closely, that detectives use them to look for clues, and that this week the class is going to become biblical detectives and investigate a murder. She tells the class to work in groups of their own choosing, read the story of Cain and Abel on page 32, and find clues which can help us explain: "Why did this murder take place?" The class goes right to work, except for Brandon, who wants to use the magnifying glass to help him read closely.

Ira the Wise and His Band of Merry Sixth-Grade Lawyers: Act One

Before the bell, Ira's classroom is controlled chaos. Kids do what they want, "As long as they are in the room, not outrageously loud about it, and as long as the activities are reasonably socially acceptable." Mr. Ira Wise and three kids are standing beside his desk, playing at the idea of starting a rap group called JWA, Jews With Attitude.

The bell rings, and Ira says one word, "Down!" It sort of works, then he says firmly, but not particularly loudly, "Everyone down, no more of this important stuff, the real learning is over, now it is my turn to teach." He smiles.

He then asks the same questions he has asked every week, "What is this class?" Everyone answers, "Jewish Law." The whole class answers at once. The answer sounds like a mechanical class answering a boring question, but if you listen carefully you know that it is more than that—there is too much energy. Rather, it is an involved class, pretending to be a bored class, playing at recreating that kind of bored classroom sound. "What do we do in this class?" Ira asks next. The whole class answers, "We learn how to act justly." Finally, Ira asks, "And what lesson will we learn again this week, that we have learned every other week?" "That justice is not easy or obvious."

"Okay my collection of junior Jewish justice-makers: Page 35, you've got five minutes to prepare the case and work out your verdicts. Do it." The students open their copies of **The Jewish Law Review** and go to work.

Chapter 4

CLASSROOM RHYTHMS
The Story of Beginnings, Middles, and Ends

*This chapter discusses the structure of lessons. It focuses on four elements: the objectives, the beginning (known in teacher-speak as **set induction**), the middle (a combination of **explaining** and **stimulus variation**), and the end (which education calls **closure**). While the job of madrikhah doesn't involve planning lessons, it does involve following and bringing life to lesson plans.*

LESSONS FROM MONDAY NIGHT FOOTBALL

Imagine for a moment that you are a blocker on a football team. That means your job is to block players from the other team and keep them from getting at your player with the football. You are not the quarterback. You aren't the one who directs the other players on the team. Still, there is a good reason for the coach to expect you to read and memorize the playbook, even if your job is just to block.

If you don't know what play the quarterback has called, then you cannot know where the football is going to be. And if you don't know where the football is going to be, you won't know whom to block in which direction. Lesson plans work the same way. You, the madrikhah, and the teacher are a team. The teacher is the quarterback, but you still need to know the playbook.

This chapter is designed to prepare you to understand your teacher's lesson plan. Armed with that knowledge, you will be prepared to fight the forces of evil and figure out what you will do as the madrikhah.

DRAWING UP THE BLUEPRINTS

In theory, every good lesson starts with a clear image of what is going to be taught. In teacher jargon, this is called setting "goals" and "objectives." Goals are generalized statements of a lesson's purpose. "Objectives" are like grids on a map; they target *exactly* what a lesson is supposed to accomplish. In classic terms, a good objective is as simple as ABCD; it is supposed to target four things.

- A = **Audience.** The objective is supposed to specifically state the nature of the learner. This is taking into consideration all of the lessons in child development we learned in the last chapter, as well as everything a teacher learns from working with her kids.

- B = **Behavior.** Objectives specify the things **learned** by a student rather than the things **taught** by the teacher. A **behavior** is something a student learns how to do (and can demonstrate in a performance).

- C = **Conditions.** This is the way the "behavior" is to be learned. It describes the activities which enable the learner to master the "behavior."

- D = **Degree.** This is the expectation of how well the student and the class will do.

Here is a classic objective:

> After having taken notes on a presentation by
> the teacher and then participating in a card
> game reviewing this information, eighty per-
> cent of students in G'veret Sabrit's sixth grade
> classroom will be able to name at least six of
> the twelve literary prophets.

Can you find the A, the B, the C, and the D?

According to the books, you plan lessons by starting with a firm idea of the "content" and "skills" you
want students to learn (behaviors) and then figure out
the activities (conditions) which will present and rein-
force this learning. That is the "theory" of how lessons
are planned, but research into "good teaching" suggests that most teachers don't work that precisely.
Often teachers start with an idea of a good activity,
and then they develop it (using good instincts and
lots of experience). Only when they are all done will
they reach a formal understanding of what a lesson
can and will accomplish.

Some teachers are artists and some teachers are
technicians. Some teachers work by instinct and some
follow theories and principles. Both ways work
(though it is much easier to teach theories and principles than to train instincts.) When you work with
your teacher, you'll probably find that he or she does a
combination of both.

Either way, a teacher does a lot of pre-class preparation. This includes not only planning, but also often
a lot of work organizing and even making the materials which will be used in that lesson. There is a lot of

pre-class work. However, once the class begins, the teacher needs: to keep in mind the timing of each component of the lesson; to always be aware of the students in relation to the learning (i.e.—are they absorbing what is being taught?); to monitor behavior; to be flexible enough to make adjustments in the plan as the situation requires.

It may have been Napoleon who said that no battle plan survives contact with the enemy. So too, lesson plans. What the teacher planned to do and what actually occurs in the classroom are often quite different due to the changing needs of the students and the spontaneity of the classroom.

I Love It When A Plan Comes Together

Now let's talk television. Most television shows begin one of two ways, both of them are hooks. Some programs use a clip, preparing you and interesting you by giving you an advanced slice of what will be happening. Other programs play out an engaging brief scene. In a murder mystery, you get the mystery before the first commercial, usually before the title sequence. They want you involved (so you won't flip to another program).

Before every commercial, something big happens. Every time they think you might turn away, or switch your attention elsewhere, they find another way of involving you.

Most shows end twice. First there is a big dramatic finish, one which resolves the plot. Then there is a commercial, then the show comes back with what they call a "tag." Sometimes, this tag is a joke which closes the experience. Sometimes, the tag is a heart-warming scene of emotions being resolved or expressed. It can be both. A third possibility is the show which doesn't end: the cliff-hanger. Here, the show is left incomplete, forcing you to come back next week.

Good lessons work a lot like television shows. It is no accident and no coincidence. Both the classroom and the television program are interested in motivating, retaining attention, and transferring information. Researchers tell us that most effective lessons contain four steps: 1) the introduction or **set induction**; 2) keeping the students' attention throughout the lesson or **stimulus variation**; 3) **explanatory**; 4) providing reinforcement through summarizing or **closure**. Television uses these same insights.

Set Induction

The purpose of **set induction** is to get the students' attention and introduce the lesson. In older educational jargon, this step was called "motivation." While one purpose of the opening activity of a lesson is "to motivate," the newer term "set induction" teaches us that the real purpose of the opening is to "induce" the "set" of thoughts and information which will be used in the lesson. We are not just "motivating" for learning; rather, we are beginning our teaching in an involving way.

The sample teachers in the prologue all use different techniques for set induction, but they share some common ideas. One thing which they share in common is a strong classroom culture. (Remember the last unit). Each of these rooms has a way of beginning, and these opening rituals are woven into set induction.

As we review these set inductions, focus in on two things: (1) the way teacher motivates student involvement and (2) the "set" of concepts or information which is introduced.

Franci's lesson begins at home. Students have prepared for this lesson with their families. They have been read the story of Esther and already know all the major characters. They have also each made or found their own noisemaker. Franci draws these two things together, by introducing a participatory retelling of the story where the noisemakers will be used. While most of the preparations were done at home or by setting up the room, Franci skillfully uses a few questions to bring these elements together and start the lesson moving.

Jane's class has already developed a set of Torah study skills. They already know a lot about how to read and interpret a biblical story. Jane's set induction is playful. The magnifying glass teaches nothing new, rather it makes a connection. It is an instant review of complex insight. The students in her room already know that the right way to read a biblical text is by "close reading." In this lesson they are going to study the story of the first murder. Jane uses the magnifying glass as a prop. The very short discussion reminds the students to read closely and sets them up to look for clues to solve a murder mystery. Whereas Franci's set induction took a whole week, with much of it happening at home, Jane's is complete in less than three minutes.

Technically, Ira's set induction is two sentences long: "Okay my collection of junior Jewish justice makers: Page 35, you've got five minutes to prepare the case and work out your verdicts. Do it." Actually, however, like Jane's, Ira's set induction is based on a continuing classroom culture. Both his opening ritual questions and the class's past experience of solving the cases in their textbook establish most of the learning context.

MIDDLING

Chapter Four: An Intermission

Franci Goldberg's Three-Ring Kindergarten: Act Two

For fifteen minutes Franci is a whirlwind. Her telling of the Esther story is a one-woman show, accompanied by a well-trained chorus of 26 six-year-olds. Franci is everywhere. She tells the story unrolling the giant scroll as she goes. She is head cheerleader, teaching their parts and gestures and then encouraging the kinder-chorus. And she is director, costuming and directing each of the students who fulfill roles in her story. She puts the king's crown on Raffi's head and leads the whole class in trumpeting "Tunt tunt tunt ta" for the king. She whispers in his ear, "Say, I want a new queen." She holds up his hand and Raffi whispers, "I want a new queen." "No," Franci says out loud, "be more kingly." And so it goes for fifteen minutes.

When she reaches "And the Jews lived happily ever after, or at least for awhile," she sits down completely exhausted. Like a perfect hand-off in a relay race, Marci, Wendy, and Michael, the two madrikhim, take over. "Okay," Marci says, "everyone to the tables." Already waiting at each chair is a copy of the **Purim is Fun Instant Lesson**. One madrikh sits at each table and works with the seven or eight students sitting there. Each of the madrikhim reads the **Instant**

Lesson section by section to his or her group. When they know the right answer, the students stick the right sticker in each square. Quietly, Franci works her way around the room, collecting the noisemakers and putting them out of the way. The reading and sticking take about 15 minutes. Just as the activity is finishing, Franci stands at the door and says clearly, "Okay everyone, line up. We're going to the kitchen to bake Hamentashen." Once again, the baton is passed.

Jane Ellen's Fourth-Grade Academy: Act Two

Jane's students work independently for four or five minutes. She and Scott, the madrikh, roam the room, checking on each group. Most of the class needs very little direction; they are used to this kind of group work, but some of the best and the worst need their strokes—and Jane and Scott are well practiced at giving them. Jane gives them a one-minute warning, and then ends the group work process.

"Before we listen to your theories about the murder of Abel, let's read the story together," Jane says. Then she breaks up the reading, "I'll be the narrator, Josh can be Cain, Lisa can read the part of God, and everyone else should read the words in bold type. The reading goes well, and the class shouts out their part, the word "brother" is heard over and over again. Jane stops the reading twice to coach Josh on his reading of Cain.

As soon as the reading is over, Jane asks, "What did you hear?" About half the class raises their hands and about half of those students answer "brother." Jane writes all the answers on the board. In a couple of quick questions, Jane and the class establish that the story teaches that "we should be our brother's keeper."

Then she says, "Let's get back to your theories about the murder." She writes the name of each group on the blackboard, and as they report, she also transcribes their theories. Then she says, "In five minutes we begin the big debate. Between now and then, collect as much evidence as you can from the story. Remember, the only proof comes from the text, and I want you to use it to prove that your theory is right." Again, the groups dive into the text. This time the noise level in the room is louder. You can hear group members arguing with each other. Jane smiles; you can tell that she is delighted.

One minute after the warning, Jane quiets the class. She says, "In this debate you should begin your arguments with one of the following, "I would like to support my theory...., I would like to dispute _____'s theory, I would like to revise my thinking." Then she gave the class three more minutes to finish their work.

Ira the Wise and His Band of Merry Sixth-Grade Lawyers: Act Two

After five minutes of work, Ira quiets the class down. The groups have been working intently. He shouts, "No more time for learning! Quiet! It is now my time to teach."

Once the class is quiet, he begins the formal teaching. "Ms. Kaufman," he begins, "can you review the facts in this case?" She starts but he interrupts her,

"Please stand, Ms. Kaufman." Cindy stands and states, "A doggie necklace made of pearls which is Dorothy's (of Kansas) disappears. She looks for it, but does not find it. She does not report the loss to the police. A year later, she sees another dog, one belonging to Mrs. H.P. Diamonds, wearing it. Mrs. Diamonds claims that the necklace was a gift. We have to decide who gets to keep the necklace." Cindy presents her verdict and explains it. Then, in succession, each of the other four groups presents its findings. In two cases, Steve in group two and for Amy in the last group, Ira gives individual students a chance to file "minority reports." As they speak, Ira makes notes on the black-board. He doesn't keep track of each of the individual groups' verdicts, instead he writes things like "Finders-keepers, losers-weepers." Soon it becomes clear that what is being recorded is his interpretation of the reasoning behind the verdict.

Making a transition, Ira says, "Let's look at how the rabbis solved a similar case." He then says, "Mr. Appleman, please read and explain the text on page 35. Eric stands up and reads, "What should be done if a person recognized his or her tools or books in another person's hands and had proof?..."

Ira stopped him and said, "Okay, explain it in your own words.

Eric said, "This is what you do when you see somebody else with your stuff which was lost or stolen."

Ira then says, "Mr. Kaufman, tell us about the 'proof' thing?" And so it goes. In about ten minutes of work, the class read the Mishnah text line-by-line and explained it in their own words. Everyone in the class understood the Mishnah's rule about when you can keep and when you must return an object which someone else has lost. Then, with a few more short questions, Ira and the group establish the basic principle on which the law was built. Finally, for this part of the lesson, they compare the "ethics" of the Mishnah's decision with the "ethics" of their own verdicts. The class reaches the conclusion that each of the verdicts is "fair in a different way?"

Ira asks, "How can two different verdicts on the same case be "fair" in different ways?" Dana answers, "Justice is a compromise—and every compromise is both fair and unfair." Then, in his best 'teacher' voice Ira asks, "And so class, what does this teach us about justice?" Then he raised his hands like a conductor and said softly, "Together." The whole class, using their impersonation of a bored class, says joyously, "Justice is not easy or obvious."

THE MIDDLE

The middle part of the lesson is probably what you would think of as the part where the teacher actually teaches. It is here that students are exposed to "new material" and are given a chance to "practice" and "master" what they are learning. Practically speaking, this middle section of the lesson involves the rotation of two different teaching skills: **stimulus variation** and **explaining**.

DIFFERENT STROKES

One way of looking at the art of teaching is called behaviorism. It sees learning as the acquisition of specific behaviors. Learning is seen as a series of "performances" which a learner becomes able to do. To a large degree, this view of teaching is the product of behavioristic psychology and much of it comes from studying white mice (and the like) in laboratories.

The word **stimulus** is an important behaviorist term. The "stimulus" is something the subject encounters; the "response" is the subject's reaction to the "stimulus." Think of it this way: If you are shocked and you pull back and say, "Ouch!", both stimulus and response are obvious.

Likewise, consider this simple lesson. The teacher shows three pictures: an apple, some honey, and a shofar. With each, she tells the Hebrew name of the object: *tapuah*, *d'vash*, and *shofar*. Then, as a drill, she shows the pictures out of order and has the class repeat the Hebrew names. Again, stimulus and response are clear. In this model of learning, learners are conditioned (trained) to perform a given behavior (response) to a particular stimulus.

Because teachers wish to keep the students involved in their lessons, **stimulus variation** is important. The skilled teacher provides a variety of learning experiences during the class session. Changing the kind of activity helps to keep learners interested. In a good classroom, there are times for the students to work alone, to be in groups (of varying sizes), for the teacher to talk or lecture, for reading, for playing, for creating, for acting, for dancing, for looking, and for finding.

There is also another reason for paying attention to stimulus variation. The research of Dr. Rita Dunn shows that different teaching methods work with different students because different students learn best in different ways. Some students learn best through hearing, some through seeing, some through writing things down themselves, and some by figuring them out themselves (etc.). By teaching the same material in more than one way (stimulus variation) we give all of the students their own best chance of succeeding.

HUH?

The other major aspect of lesson presentation is called **explaining**. (Can you guess the meaning of this technical term?) Explaining is the clarification of any idea, procedure, or process. Clear explanations are vital. A fuzzy or incomplete explanation can cause confusion, anxiety, or even total loss of attention.

One way that a teacher can check his/her explanation skills is to simply ask. "Got it?"

As we review the middle portion of our three model lessons, look carefully for the two important elements: (1) stimulus variation, and (2) explaining.

Franci runs a hyperactive preschool talk show. Her room is a constant flow of activity, yet, when we look at it, it is carefully balanced. The first part of the class involves Franci's one-person Purim performance. Even as she leads the ensemble performance of the Purim story, she is offering a variety of constantly interweaving stimuli. There is a giant scroll on the board which can be read and which has pictures. There is her telling of the story which can be both heard and seen. (Yes, she overacts. Yes, she overacts on purpose.) There are the costumes and props which can be seen and touched. There are the noisemakers which can be touched and heard. Even in this direct presentation, these stimuli are all interwoven.

Then, the action shifts. Using the sticker **Instant Lesson** Franci and her madrikhim completely change the learning style. The work is now being quietly done in ones and twos. Here the explaining is not a carnival-like flow, but a direct reading of each part of the story, matched by choosing and placing the correct sticker in the correct box. Finally, Franci moves the class to the kitchen for the third part of the lesson. This time food (something you can taste) becomes the center of a third retelling of the story.

Jane's lesson involves constant changes in the groupings used for instruction. It starts with small group work, then merges the class into a performance troupe, allows Jane to do some "frontal teaching," and then has the class return to small group exploration. All of this happens in about twenty minutes.

Likewise, the kind of learning is also changing constantly. First students read and discuss in small groups. The "explaining" is something they do for each other. Formally, this kind of learning is called "discovery" learning because students discover the reasons on their own. Next, the class does an oral reading where the use of the word "brother" is made clear both through the graphics in the text (reading) and through the oral reading (hearing).

The third part of the lesson involves explaining through the careful asking of questions. Students are led to explain the story's lesson through a carefully structured series of questions. This is called Socratic teaching. Socrates was a famous Greek philosopher who trained his students in ideas through questions and answers. Socratic teaching is a favorite teacher style. Jane also makes careful use of the blackboard. By writing down the students' theories, Jane makes concepts visual.

Finally, by returning students to the small groups, Jane again returns the responsibility for explaining this biblical text back to the students.

In many ways, Ira's lesson is similar to Jane's. It involves a combination of small group discovery learning and whole class involvement in Socratic discussions. It also involves the special dynamic of text reading. Here the text to be studied is read one line at a time and the whole group works together to explain it. In Ira's lesson the central activity is explaining and all members of the class participate. If you look carefully, you will again see a good balance of seeing and hearing, and of explaining and discovering.

CLOSING

Chapter Four: an Epilogue

Franci Goldberg's Three-Ring Kindergarten: Act Two

"Quick!" Franci says as the class comes back from the kitchen. "We only have a few minutes left before we have to leave and I want to go over everything we learned today." She picks up the three-cornered hat and the beard and asks, "Who am I?" Everyone screams "Haman." Jason goes "Boooo!" and everyone joins in. Next she picks up the crown and the sceptre and in answer to her question, the class screams "The King." In turn, Franci dresses herself as Esther and Mordechai. Then with the help of the madrikhim, each child is sent out of the room with his/her noise-maker, hamantash, and finished sticker Instant Lesson. As they leave, Franci says, "See you all at the Megillah reading."

Jane Ellen's Fourth-Grade Academy: Act Two

After the big debate, the class establishes that Cain was angry or jealous that God accepted Abel's sacrifice and not his. In addition, Jon, who has a younger brother, thought that Cain was angry because Adam and Eve gave his younger brother, Abel, all of the attention. Then, Jane asked her last question, "What do you think is the most important sentence in this story?" Quickly, the class agrees on "Am I my brother's keeper?"

Next, Jane has the class open up their **Being Torah Student Commentaries**. Each student writes his or her own ending to a comment which begins: "To be a good 'keeper,' a person should..." After two minutes of work, Jane invites students to share their answers. She writes them on the board. Then she asks the students to pick comments by other students which they really like. They all copy their favorite second comments into their **Student Commentary**. Jane ends the lesson by saying, "Thanks for all the Torah you guys taught me today. I learned a lot."

Ira the Wise and His Band of Merry Sixth-Grade Lawyers: Act Two

Heading into the stretch, Ira tells his class, "Well my junior justice-makers, the time has come to figure out what you've learned." Without waiting, the class moans in unison, "Justice is not easy or obvious." Ira smiled, and then said, "Right but wrong. Now turn to page 37 and work through the two text cases. If you can do these, you've got the point."

Next comes five minutes of work, then there is a short discussion. This time when someone gets the right answer, Ira says, "Right." As the bell rings, Ira says, "No one moves." Then he says, "What is this class?" Every answers, "Jewish Law." "What do we do in this class?" Ira asks next. The whole class answers, "We learn how to act justly." Finally, Ira asks, "And what lesson will we learn again this week, that we have learned every other week?" "That justice is not easy or obvious." As his closing comment Ira says, "Anyone who wants to audition for JWA stay after class, otherwise, get out of here!"

THE FINISHING TOUCHES

You have undoubtedly heard—or perhaps used—the expression "saved by the bell." That is not a phrase that can be allowed to exist in the teacher's vocabulary. If the lesson ends because the bell rings, then it is quite likely that nothing attempted that day will be "saved" by the students. The teacher needs to put **closure** (the fourth aspect) on the lesson. Closure is more than just a planned ending, it is a drawing together of a lesson—bringing it to a close.

Teachers use closure to help the students draw together all of the lesson's elements. Closure is the part of the lesson where students make sense out of the session, when a teacher helps the students organize their thinking concerning the materials studied that day.

There is a Hebrew word that is very useful at this point—*sikkum*. A sikkum is a summary or a review. And that is what closure is all about. A sikkum might include a review of the main points of a lecture; asking the students to recap the activities that the class performed; asking the students to apply what they learned during the session to some situation, problem, or question.

As we review the closures used by our three model teachers, think about two things: (1) how students are enabled to bring the lesson together, and (2) what the student will take from this lesson.

Franci ends her lesson by using the costumes and props to review the names of the four major characters in the Purim story. She then sends students home with a *hamantash* and a worksheet, both of which review the lesson. She also expects most of her class to show up for the congregational *Megillah* reading, the ultimate reinforcement.

Jane's class ends with a short summation and then a ceremony. Each student writes a comment, then each student records one other student's comment. Finally, as she does every week, Jane thanks the class for teaching her.

Ira's class ends by testing students' understanding of the *Mishnah* by applying it to two new cases. Once the specific lesson is over, Ira ends the class with a ritual which emphasizes the course's major lesson.

BEGINNINGS, MIDDLES, AND MEANS TO THE END

Like a television show, a good lesson tries to hold the students' attention and keep them from tuning out or changing their channels. To achieve their goals, both good TV production teams and great teachers use certain patterns and rhythms. They "hook" involvement and "set" a series of expectations, they slowly unfold their stories while constantly changing the stimulus, and they conclude by giving you a sense of the whole. **Set Induction**, **Stimulus Variation**, **Explanation**, and **Closure** have been part of your life for a long time. Now you can recognize them.

We began this chapter with the metaphor of a football player. We suggested that even if you are just a lineman, knowing the play helps you know which way to block. Likewise, as a madrikhah, understanding the rhythm of a lesson lets you know how to help. In the sample lessons used in this chapter you've seen some excellent examples. Franci and her team of madrikhim function as a tag team. When Franci is "on" her madrikhim move into their "zone defense" and insure her success by influencing and controlling the class. When Franci "hands off the ball" they are in position, ready to work with small groups. Meanwhile, Franci is back playing "safety" and dealing with individual students. Their knowledge of Franci's lesson pattern lets them automatically be in the right place at the right time. Jane and Scott have a similar understanding. While Jane never relinquishes control of the class to him, Scott, too, has his teaching moments. At the right moments, he leaves his corner post and moves into one-on-one and small group tutorials. Other times, he serves as a "rear guard" letting Jane continue teaching while he handles special problems.

Okay, now that you know the play, play ball.

CASE STUDIES

Here are the beginnings of three lessons. Read them. Decide which elements are part of the "motivation" for the class, which elements "include the set" of understandings the lesson will use, and which are not productive. Evaluate these beginnings.

Case 1

Rivka is at her desk working. As the fourth grade students come in, they go to their proper places. On the board is the list of things the class will do along with the time each activity is expected to take. Some students come over and say, "Hello." When they do, Rivka gives them a big smile and says "Shalom." Then she goes back to her paperwork. When the bell rings, Rivka takes attendance. She calls off each name and has a short interchange with each student. When the business is complete, she stands up and moves to the center of the room, her "teaching position."

Rivka begins, "Today, class, I want to start this lesson by talking about birthdays. I want to know what you do on your birthday. Susan, what do you do on your birthday?" Susan gives a short explanation which emphasizes the presents she received. Next Rivka asks James the same question. He tells about the baseball game that he took his friends to as his party. James, too, lists all the presents he received. Rivka is democratic; she lets everyone in the class describe their birthday rituals. The emphasis in almost every presentation is on the number of gifts received. This takes about twelve minutes.

Next Rivka asks, "Why do we do all these things on our birthdays?" A few hands are raised, and when each student is called on, he or she gives a short answer: "It is fun!" "It is a tradition." "To make it special." After each answer Rivka says, "Good."

Then she reviews. "We do special things on our birthdays to make them stand out from other days. We have birthday traditions because they help us make that day special." Then she says, "Rosh Ha-Shanah is the 'birthday of the world.' Who knows what traditions we use to make Rosh Ha-Shanah special?"

Case 2

Nate, the teacher, leaves a shofar on his desk. Before class begins, his kids are busy blowing it and having contests. Nate monitors things, answering questions when necessary, but pretty well staying out of things. Meanwhile Adina, the madrikhah, sits on the other side of the room. She has the attendance book open. Quietly, without saying a word, she checks students as they walk in. While one of the kids keeps score on the blackboard, Stephanie beats out David's record *Tekiyah Gedolah* with a 48-second effort.

When Nate senses that it is time to begin, he sends kids to their seats and quietly calms them down. He says, "Clear off your desks. I want to start today's lesson with a mystery.

He pulls a crumpled sheet of yellow legal paper out of his briefcase.

"I found this slip of paper yesterday. It was in a box of things my great grandmother brought from Poland.

I want you to help me figure it out."

Ilene interrupts and asks, "Is this real or is this another one of your teacher tricks?"

Nate smiles and says, "Don't ask." Then he goes on, "When I opened up the piece of paper, I saw that it was a list. I made photocopies of the list for you. I want to know if you can help me figure out what it means."

Things to change:
1. I yelled at my wife when I was really mad at myself.
2. I told my daughter, "I'm busy now but I'll make time for you later." But I forgot.
3. I promised myself that I would lose weight but I still ate too much at dinner.
4. I talk about myself too much.
5. I forgot to take out the garbage.
6. I still haven't gone over to talk to Raphael to see if there is anything I can do for him now that he lost his job.

There are sixty-two items on the list. The list is signed, Levi Yitzhak. Nate asks the class to break into groups and see if they can figure out the purpose of this list. He gives them three minutes. They ask for more time, but he says, "We're in a hurry—too much to teach today."

Quickly each group voices its theory. Then Nate says, "I took the letter to the rabbi who was very interested. He asked me to wait a minute while he looked something up. After looking in five or six books and keeping me waiting for ten minutes, he said, 'This may be a very important list.' Then he handed me this story." The story Nate then reads comes from Martin Buber's *Tales of the Hasidim*. It begins "Every night Rabbi Levi Yitzḥak would go up to his room and make a list of the things which he had done wrong during the day. It ends with the rabbi saying, "Last night when Levi Yitzḥak promised that none of these sins would ever be repeated, he was a liar, but tonight Levi Yitzḥak will tell the truth."

The class discusses the story and quickly Nate introduces the word t'shuvah, repentance. So begins his lesson on Rosh Ha-Shanah. For its culmination, Nate will ask, "How does the sound of the shofar help us to do t'shuvah?

Case 3

Barbara leaves attendance-taking for the middle of her class. It is something she does when students are working in groups. She begins her lesson this way. "I know you've been taught a lot about Rosh Ha-Shanah and I'm not going to take a lot of time repeating. You all know that it is the Jewish New Year, the beginning of the High Holidays and the Days of Awe. You also know that it is a time when you begin a process called t'shuvah, repentance. Who can define 'repentance?'

The class contributes some definitions and Barbara writes them on the board. She then says, "*T'shuvah* is not an easy thing to define. It is also not an easy thing to do."

She passes out a photocopy of a definition of t'shu-vah written by Maimonides. In three sentences, she reminds the class of who Maimonides was, and then begins the process of reading and discussing his definition.

Compare these three set inductions.

BRAINSTORMING

1. The students in the first grade are going to have a special Shabbat celebration in their classroom and invite their parents to attend. Outline how you would explain this project to the class and give them the details of what they are going to have to do in order to prepare for this event.

2. A fourth-grade class of 18 children is learning about the geography of Israel. Make a list of as many different ways you can think of to teach Israeli geography to this class. Which methods would you choose? Why?

3. Mrs. Haim is finishing a session teaching about bar/bat Mitzvah for a fifth-grade class. They have been learning about the history of bar/bat mitzvah, how it is celebrated, what the requirements are in this community for bar/bat mitzvah. Suggest ways for her to bring closure to this lesson.

4. You are the madrikhah in the fourth-grade class, which is about to study the story of Jonah. The teacher has asked you to prepare a way of introducing the story. She wants you to emphasize why the story of Jonah is important today. Come up with at least three "beginnings" for this lesson.

Journal Entry

OPTION 1

Have your principal request lesson plans for the next week from the teachers in all of the classes. As a group, analyze the lesson plans. Someone should record the group's answers in writing.

1. What are the teacher's goals for the lesson?
2. How does the teacher plan to perform the set induction? How might you do it differently?
3. What methods does the teacher plan to use to teach the lesson? Are they varied? What other methods might you use?
4. How does the teacher plan to explain and bring closure? Do you have any suggestions?
5. What do you think the Madrikhah's role should be during each part of the lesson?

After answering those questions, each madrikhah should take the answers for the class they will be observing when the lesson plan you have analyzed will be taught. Observe that class for at least one half-hour. After you have completed your observations, share your findings with your fellow madrikhim.

1. Compare as many of the answers to questions 1-4 as possible (within the allotted thirty minutes) with what actually happens. What changes were made from the lesson plan during the actual class period? Why do you think

that they were made? Do you agree with the changes?

2. Watch the interactions between the teacher and the students and among the students. How many times does the teacher ask a question? How many times do students ask questions? How many times do students talk to one another?

3. If you were the regular madrikhah in that class, what would you be doing during that thirty minutes?

OPTION 2

Choose a class to observe, perhaps your own. Do not discuss it with the teacher. Instead, just watch the lesson and take notes. See if you can figure out the following things.

1. What are the goals of the lesson?
2. What are the distinct activities?
3. What was the purpose of each activity?

After the lesson, sit down with the teacher and compare your notes with the prepared lesson plan. You will both learn a lot from the experience.

COMMANDMENTS FOR MADRIKHOT

NEGATIVE COMMANDMENTS

1. Never forget the overall game plan. Even if there is a moment when you aren't needed, remember you may be important to the next activity.

2. Never assume that each student understands the material or instructions in the same way. If one of them seems confused or lost, simply ask them if they understand.

3. Don't get so caught up in one activity that you forget the rest of the world. Once in a while glance towards the teacher and around the room so you can be aware of everyone's needs.

4. Don't learn too much from this lesson. Even if you now think that you can second guess your teacher and plan a better class (every madrikhah reaches that point for a while)—keep it to yourself, or share it after class. You'll get your chance when you do grow up to be a Jewish teacher.

POSITIVE COMMANDMENTS

1. Know the playbook. Keep the flow of the lesson in mind. Use your understanding of classroom rhythms to anticipate where you will next be needed.

2. Always remember that lesson plans are flexible. Be prepared to go with the flow and follow the teacher's lead.

Journal Entry

This journal assignment is designed to get you ready for your session on classroom management. In advance we want you to know that different teachers work differently—that's why we're asking you to gather a number of opinions.

Please interview three teachers in your school regarding their thoughts about classroom management and good discipline procedures. After you have conducted the three interviews, share your findings with the other madrikhim in the school.

Some of the questions you should ask the teachers are:

1. Does this school have a specific philosophy of classroom management, or are there important school rules which affect the way you run your classroom?

2. What specific rules and regulations do you have for your class? How do you enforce them?

3. What should be the role of the madrikh regarding classroom management?

4. When do you involve parents in solving behavior problems? How do you do it?

THE MANAGEMENT ALL-STARS

A Prologue to Chapter Five

1

It was the second week of school. Class had just begun. Mrs. Vatik was writing on the board; her back was to the fifth grade. There was a very soft noise, the sound of a Reebok falling on a tile square.

Without turning around, Mrs. Vatik said, "Russel Siegle, get back in your seat. I've told you before that Mrs. Vatik is a mean old lady teacher who has been putting up with sugar-dosed Hebrew school brats for twelve years. She knows tricks you haven't even thought of yet. She catches everyone. I have already warned you that you can't get away with anything in her class. If you do your work, then you'll get a party and lots of treats, but whether you like it or not, in this classroom you are going to work, and you are going to do your best work. And Mr. James M. Kaufman, before I turn around and catch you, put away the comic book. If I see it, I will add it to my collection. All mean old lady teachers have eyes in the back of their heads. Now Russel, read the first line on page 25, and do it brilliantly, with your own special panache."

2

On the first day of class Mike passed out the class rules to his class. He spent nearly a half-hour going over them. Students were required to sign the class-room behavior contract and then take it home for their parents to sign. The first fifteen minutes of the second session were devoted to reviewing the rules, then Mike got down to business.

Now it was November. Class had begun. Most of the class had settled down to work. In ones and twos they were completing workbook pages 58, 59 and 61. Jamie was staring out the window and Gregg was whispering to Evan. Mike walked over and stood near Jamie. He didn't say a word. He just stood near him and looked. Jamie felt the pressure. He opened his book. Greg took a balled-up piece of paper, stood up, shot it like a basketball into the wastebasket, and then shouted, "Two points." Mike walked up to the board and wrote Greg's name on it. Greg sat down. He knew that if he got out of hand again, things would move to step three.

3

To understand the way Aaron teaches you need to get there at least twenty minutes before the kids do. When Aaron hits the front doors of the school his hands are full; it is always better if someone else is there to open the door. Usually he is carrying a box overflowing with things, a bag or two, and his knapsack, which usually has so much in it that it will not close. If no one is there, Aaron leans the box against one side of the door, fumbles the other side of the door open with a hand, catches the open door with his foot, and then quickly grabs the box before it topples.

When Aaron hits the classroom, he begins unpacking. He doesn't quite know where everything goes, but he finds a way of laying it out so that some things are hidden, some are very obvious, and anything he wants can be found in an instant. As he works, he stops to look at each handout, each object, each resource. If you watch quietly (and don't disturb him) you can see the joy of rediscovery as he finds something interesting in each piece. About ten minutes before the first of his third-graders show, Alan and Debi, his madrikhim, check in. Immediately, Aaron starts showing the madrikhim the various things they may use in the course of the day. Most teachers who make lesson plans write outlines. When Aaron writes down his plans they look more like family trees; they contain all kinds of branching options. Aaron also uses these moments like a basketball coach, outlining the blocks and picks his guards should set during the lesson.

You've seen the pre-game, now this is Aaron in action. Fifteen minutes into the lesson, Aaron has finished introducing the new Hebrew letter of the week, *Lammed.* He asks the students to open up their *Alef Bet Gimmel Dalet* books and trace the letter. While Debi and Alan roam the room, helping individual students with their work and monitoring progress, Aaron makes a point of sitting down and working with Brian, Jessica and Sean. He gathers them to his desk. Brian has missed two sessions in a row, Jessica has some learning difficulties, and Sean has a hard time focusing without supervision. While most of the rest of the students work through the material with only a little bit of help from the madrikhim, Aaron reteaches the introduction and works through two pages with his tutorial group.

Suddenly, if you listen closely, you realize the working buzz in the room has changed, just a little bit. Everyone is still working, but within perhaps a minute or two, boredom will set in with a few of the more restless students. Without warning, Aaron shouts, "Stop! Nobody move. I'm getting bored with the workbooks. I think it's time for a game." He gets up and walks over to his knapsack, takes out three brown envelopes. He tosses one across the room to Alan and says, "Table One." Aaron walks over and hands the second to Debi (she is notorious for dropping things he tosses). He makes a big deal out of handing it to her and everyone laughs. He says, "Debi, sit between Justin and Roger and run table two. Susan and Maxine, if you'll move your chairs up to my table, we'll be the third game. The directions are inside. Play for a few minutes and then my table will challenge the other two for the first round of the *Alef Bet Gimmel Dalet* olympics." Everyone shouts "Yea!" and then gets back to work.

4

Bill held up the green twisted candle and said, "It's almost three quarters burned down. With another two or three good class sessions I'll owe you a pizza party." Then he took out his old Korean War Zippo lighter and kindled the flame.

Then he began the lesson. Once, about a half-hour later, when Brent started goofing off and Brad seemed ready to join him, Bill walked over towards the flame. Before he got there, Jenifer said, "You guys are going to spoil it. Mr. K. will blow it out and it will take us even longer to earn the party." The lesson went on.

Chapter 5

CLASSROOM MANAGEMENT

Classroom management is the part of teaching which has to do with "control." In this unit you will learn that there are many different workable ways of "controlling" a class. You will also learn something of the strategy of effective madrikhim placement.

THE ONE-MINUTE MANAGER

Language teaches some important lessons. We learn one from the title of this chapter, "Classroom Management." What it doesn't say speaks volumes. It doesn't say "discipline." "Classroom management" is the latest education lingo for what used to be called "discipline." The change isn't just one of vocabulary—it reflects new insights. Discipline is a way of coping with behavior problems that interrupt the flow of learning; management is the art of structuring a classroom environment that contributes to and supports learning. Discipline is a minor component of classroom management.

Management implies a proactive (there is that word again!), constructive approach—rather than responding to "situations" as they occur.

ZONE-DEFENSE VERSUS MAN-TO-MAN

Every teacher has his or her own theory about "classroom management." They will tell you such sage pieces of conventional wisdom as "start out strict..." While there are hundreds of theories, basically they break down into two schools of management, those who center on "rules" and those who focus on "instructional planning." As a student, you are an expert at how teachers successfully and unsuccessfully try to control you. As you read about the major schools of classroom management, think of examples of each strategy.

"Assertive discipline" is sort of the classroom version of "Tough Love." It represents the "rule" side of the spectrum. It believes that the teacher working with his class (and often with the parents) establishes clear, precise rules for acceptable and even good behavior. Often, in this kind of classroom, rewards for great work and good behavior are as important as punishments. In addition, teacher, students, and parents understand the consequences of any given pattern of behavior.

Classically, in a classroom using **assertive discipline**, the first time you do something wrong your name is written on the board (as a warning). If you do something else wrong, there is an internal punishment (like extra work). The third time, the principal is involved, and the fourth time parents are contacted, etc.

Assertive discipline is a "contract" system where everyone knows the rules, and where the teacher is "fair," handing out rewards and warnings based on commonly understood rules. In **assertive discipline**, the student is urged to take responsibility for his own actions, because he knows the consequences of those actions. While many educators have used systems of this kind, **Lee and Marlene Kantor** are the names most associated with this school.

Instructional Management is the opposite end of the spectrum. Rather than setting expectations for student behavior, it emphasizes the things that teachers can do to prevent the need for "discipline." It suggests that by effectively planning interesting lessons, carefully controlling the classroom environment, smoothly changing from one activity to another (without big pauses), and being sensitive to what is happening to individual students within the classroom, teachers can prevent most situations that would ultimately call for a disciplinary intervention.

In a classic classroom using **instructional management**, the teacher does three things. First, he pays careful attention to the room set-up. Desks are placed where students can easily focus on and be involved in the lesson. Seating set-ups which allow students to disengage are eliminated. Likewise, careful attention is paid to the placement of students (who should or should not sit next to whom) and the positioning of staff. Second, the teacher plans his lesson in terms of involvement. He anticipates the length of time students will actively be engaged in any given activity, and then finds a way to shift into a new activity at the point where students will begin "tuning out." Third, the teacher who uses **instructional management** functions with his radar up, ready to perceive any frustration or difficulty students are having with the lesson.

Whereas **assertive discipline** makes the student live up to a set of expectations (which are often mutually set), in **instructional management**, the teacher accepts much of the responsibility for creating a learning situation which constantly involves the students. **Assertive discipline** believes that developing a student's sense of self-control is the best way of managing the classroom. **Instructional management** believes that most problems in classroom behavior stem from the failure of a lesson to engage the students—that when things are boring, too difficult, too easy, unclear, etc., children tend to have trouble controlling themselves. **Jacob Kounin** is probably the leading "rebbe" of the **instructional management** school.

Two other strategies are worth mentioning. **Carl Rogers** is a famous humanist psychologist who did some writing about the classroom. He suggests that the communications between teacher and student are the key to management. When there is a real relationship between teacher and student, classroom problems are easy to solve. **Rogers** suggests that a teacher must communicate "realness" (he says that enthusiasm and boredom are both examples of "realness,") acceptance, and empathetic understanding. **Dr Hayim Ginott**, another child psychologist, contributes to this school of thought by suggesting that when the teacher needs to correct a student, he should criticize the student's action, not the student himself. (E.g., "I really don't like it when you drop your books on the floor" as opposed to "I really don't like you when you drop your books on the floor." For both of these humanistic psychologists, classroom management centers on relationships (not rules or activities).

The other humanist strategy which is also very popular is **classroom democracy**. While you can see an element of **classroom democracy** in the planning phase of **assertive discipline**, real **classroom democracy** (as popularized by **Rudolf Dreikurs**) involves students not only in setting the rules, but in solving problems. In the **assertive discipline** model, teachers take responsibility once the rules are set; in **classroom democracy** the students are constantly involved in redefining the way the classroom functions.

As a student and as a madrikh, you probably have your own preferred classroom management style. You also probably have experienced good teachers and good classes which use differing models. All of this is Okay. Some schools have particular philosophies of management and some leave it up to the individual teacher. That is the nature of schools and classrooms.

You may wonder why we went to the trouble of using technical terms and noting the theoreticians. That question is simply answered. You are now part of a profession. Learning its language and history will help you to communicate with other teachers, learn from professional literature, and understand that you need not invent everything you do in the classroom. Teachers, especially Jewish teachers, have a heritage from which to work.

A FEW BASIC TRUTHS

As a madrikh, you will not determine the management style used in your classroom (though, depending on the teacher, you may have influence). You will have to adapt yourself to the environment established by the teacher. Regardless of the school of management chosen (or the personal style utilized) the following insights will tend to be true:

1. There will be fewer "discipline problems" during good lessons than during unclear or unfocused teaching.

2. Transitions are one of the more problematic areas. The more quickly and smoothly the class moves from one activity to the next, the less "difficulty" will be experienced.

3. It is important to be "fair." Kids talk about teachers being either "fair" or "mean." (This is not the same as "strict" or "easy.") Being "fair," which means somehow being both consistent and able to take special situations into consideration, is important.

4. Good relationships with students are another key to classroom management. Mutual trust and respect help a lot.

5. Classroom management needs to be holistic. It involves more than the classroom. It needs to fit with the school environment and the administration, and it needs to work with parents and their expectations.

EVEN GREAT MANAGEMENT ISN'T PERFECT

Many classroom "discipline problems" can be prevented, but not all of them can. A good teacher, carefully teaching a well-planned lesson, can avoid many classroom issues, but not all of them. There are at least three kinds of problems that no preparation can avoid:

* Students who have great difficulty in controlling themselves in any setting, will occasionally fail to control themselves in any class, *though with good management these disturbances can be limited and contained.*

* Classes at the beginning of the year, especially older classes, will test teachers—that's part of the ritual. *World-class teachers score easy victories during this round.*

* Certain days are just "one of those days" when "the natives are restless." Whether generated by the weather, the horoscope, the proximity to vacation, or a local world series victory, even the best teachers sometimes have to teach while swimming upstream.

THE BEST DEFENSE

Now let's talk about madrikhim. Most people learn how to be a parent by having been a child. Most people learn about being a teacher by having been a student. Madrikhim are new elements in the Jewish classroom. Most of your teachers never had madrikhim working in classrooms where they were students. They, too, may have a lot to learn, because

114

all over North America, teachers are just learning how to use madrikhim effectively. Here are at least three ways that madrikhim can enhance classroom management:

Coverage: The Rudy-the-Rabbit Story

Like Rudy, the kid in the first *Meatballs* movie, you are smaller, faster, sneakier, and cleverer—YOU are Rudy-the-Rabbit. (Even if you don't know the movie, you'll still understand).

Picture this: The students are sitting in a clump on the floor, and the teacher is telling the story of Esther and Mordekhai. You, the Madrikh (Rudy-the-Rabbit) are sitting on the floor, too.

You are not sitting on the edge of the group, and you are not lying on your back. You are sitting in the middle of that clump of students. Joey, who's been a little overzealous all day, is behind you and to the right. You don't even need to lean over to touch his knee, and you have a direct line of sight to shoot your "evil eye" at Susie just as she begins to whisper to Heather. Little person-to-person defenses like these don't distract the teacher or the other students, and don't draw attention to the potential offenders. This is called **coverage**—positioning yourself so that you can physically or visually reach a large number of students without interrupting the flow of the lesson.

The Captain of Time-Out

Sometimes, being asked to leave the room is a punishment. Sometimes, it is a privilege. And, sometimes, leaving the room is a normal part of classroom life. As a madrikh, you are capable of working with students in a corner or in the corridor. You are the person in the classroom who can take an overexcited student into the hall for a one-to-one tutorial, or give a confused student an extra explanation, or do something special with the two kids who finished their work early.

We know that good classroom management means prevent frustration resulting from confusion—you have the ability to work one-on-one to make things clear.

We know that good management means providing a secure environment for learning. You are one resource in the classroom, who can help the teacher enhance the environment by working with a single student or a small group.

You can also use your extra eyes and ears to give needed extra attention to a student who may need it. Sometimes, just sitting next to little Shmuelik—who is having a bad day—and coloring your own **Do-It-Yourself Megillah** can help him feel a whole lot better. Because of the relationship that you will establish (or already have established) with your students, having your companionship can have a very positive result.

Joe Madrikh, Professional Friend

Another vital aspect of good classroom management is a knowledge of the students as individual human beings. You can gain this knowledge by attempting to build a solid relationship with the students during school time. Students will respond to a madrikh or a teacher who shows a personal interest in them. Students want the teaching team to see them as people who are real and have a life outside of the classroom.

Sometimes, profound caring can be a school's most important message.

CASE STUDIES

ROUND ONE: THE BASICS

The following cases are simple, but they involve some management concepts. Discuss what the madrikh should do in each case.

1. Mrs. Epstein, your teacher, is a little late. You are the first staff member to enter your classroom. As you enter, Roger and Stuart are busy setting the classroom clock ahead fifteen minutes.

2. Michael and Joe, in the two seats at the end of the row, continue to talk to one another.

3. Mr. Frank passes out a worksheet and asks students to work in groups of no more than three. The students quickly break up and go to work. No one is raising their hands. No one is causing trouble.

4. Michele, the substitute, is trying to lead the sixth-grade class in a discussion of why Jews wear a tallit. Everyone is giving her a hard time. Finally, when things get out of hand, Sharon, an extra madrikhah whom the principal assigned to help out, shouts over the kids talking over Michele, "Will you all please be quiet and listen to Michele!" What should you, the regular madrikh, do?

5. Mr. Goldenberg is carrying on a discussion with a small group of students on the left side of the room. In the back, two students are throwing paper at each other. The first time, you walk over and quietly ask them to behave reasonably. Almost as soon as you turn around, they start in again.

6. Mr. Temple is leading a lecture discussion about the prophet Amos. Most of the class is listening. The discussion is going well. Sean is doodling on his blue jeans. He may or may not be listening, but no one else is being disturbed. Josh is in the back row, obviously doing his math homework, but when Mr. Temple asks a question, his hand goes up. You, the madrikh, are sitting on the side counter.

The Challenge Round

These management problems are more difficult. To solve these, you need to first figure out what the teacher should do, and then discuss what the madrikh should do. You may also need to involve the school principal and even parents in your solution.

Case 1

From the moment Keith walks into Hebrew school, it is clear that he is mad. Usually, Keith is a fairly happy if sneaky child, the kind that is busy pleasing the teacher while getting someone else in trouble. Today, he walks in, puts his head down on the desk, and doesn't communicate at all. When the teacher tries to involve him in the lesson, Keith's responses alternate between an empty, almost silent, "Okay, whatever you say," and an angry snap, "Why do I have to do it—I don't feel like it." Twenty minutes into the lesson, you find him tearing into confetti one of the paintings left on the wall by the day school who shares the room. Keith's mother is the treasurer of the Temple and the former chair of the education committee.

Case 2

This seventh grade is the ultimate Hebrew School class from hell, fourteen boys and two girls who have all been together since their parents helped to build the synagogue. It is the second week in October, and they are about to receive their third teacher. The first teacher left after one session, she clearly wasn't cut out for the job. The second one lasted three weeks, and after five complaints from parents, and three special meetings with the educator, it was decided to move her down to the fourth grade. The educator, herself, covered the class for two sessions. Now, a new team of one teacher and one madrikh is being brought in. The class is looking forward to the challenge. They have already started a pool on how long this teacher will last.

Case 3

Darsey is the son of a Jewish mother and a non-Jewish father. In his early years, he went to a Christian Sunday school. Later, his mother divorced his father and remarried a Jewish marine. He is one tough dude. He decided that "his Jewish son," was going to be raised as a "Jew." So, at age eleven, Darsey was sent to Hebrew school.

From day one, Darsey told everyone at Hebrew school that he was a Christian and that he didn't belong there. All his actions suggested that he didn't belong there. But, because everyone was scared of the punishments that Darsey might receive, no one called his home. When Darsey was twelve, the rabbi called a big conference of parents, rabbi, educator, and teacher. They decided that Darsey had to be given a choice as whether or not he wanted to be a Jew and whether or not he wanted to have a Bar Mitzvah. Darsey surprised everyone, and chose to stay in school and have the ceremony.

Even when Darsey decided to get down to work, it was still just about impossible. He has reading problems and tremendous difficulty in sitting still and focusing. With much patience from everyone, he made it through.

Much to everyone's even greater surprise, a year later, Darsey shows up for the first night of Hebrew High School. He has one side of his head shaved with a paper clip as an earring. He is carrying a skateboard which he has spray-painted to read "Suicidal Potential" (the name of a local punk rock cult band). Within twenty minutes, Darsey bounces in and out of four different elective classes. What should be done?

COMMANDMENTS FOR MADRIKHIM

NEGATIVE COMMANDMENTS

1. Never sit alone at the back or side of the group. Whenever possible, place yourself in a location which will improve the lesson.

2. Don't scream "Shut up" or "Sit down" from the back of the room.

3. Don't forget that people can change. Never form a final expectation that a student won't behave, or will always fail—continually give your students room to live up to your expectations.

4. Don't expect students to behave well if the teaching you are doing is unplanned or unclear.

5. Don't think that you are the last defense. Remember, management is holistic. Your teacher, the principal, and the students' parents are all part of the team.

6. Don't be afraid to ask for help.

7. Never assume that if you are not specifically leading an activity, you have nothing to do.

POSITIVE COMMANDMENTS

1. Be fair (not mean). Be consistent (not inflexible).

2. Know and respect each student.

3. Practice good coverage.

4. When "correcting" a student, always separate the action from the person.

5. Work hard to make transitions quick and easy. Don't leave spaces where focus wanders.

CLASSROOM CONVERSATIONS

A Prologue to Chapter 6

1

In the hall outside of class, Joyce asks, "How's the python?"

Rob smiles, "Back at my father's house, Mom won't let me keep it in our apartment. Putting it in her bed was not a good idea!"

"Probably not!"

Rob smiles again.

2

Sandy is a little bit nervous. She isn't so sure that she wants to lead a discussion group with twelve twelve-year-olds. Twelve was just four years ago for her, and Sandy remembers some of the groups that her friends disrupted then.

She looks down at the sheet of paper which reads, "Sikhah Notes" and reviews what she is supposed to do. Step One says, "Go around the circle and have everyone introduce him or herself. REMEMBER: MAKE *EYE* CONTACT." Sandy does just that, and surprisingly it is fun. She asks a boy named Shane if his mother named him after the Alan Ladd movie. When he says, "Yes," she tells him, "I love to stay up late when it is on TV and cry my eyes out." Everyone laughs. She also establishes that Arnold Kaufman's dad owns the deli and that Jack is Shana Fried's little brother.

Next the Sikhah Notes instruct her, "ASK EVERYONE: What modern sin do you think is the hardest to stop doing? MAKE *EVERYONE* ANSWER." Sandy asks the question, and again goes around the circle.

The answers come back almost as the sheet predicted: "Drugs," "Cocaine," "Drugs," "Killing Someone," "Drinking," "Drugs," "Nintendo," "Drugs."

Next, the sheet reads, "Step three: "Establish that most of these sins which are difficult to stop are addictive." Sandy asks, "We've made an interesting list of modern sins. What do they all have in common?"

Eric: "They are all sins?"

Sandy: "Right, but what makes most of them hard to stop?"

Rachel: "They are addictive."

Sandy: "Good. But, Rachel, what's 'addictive'?"

In four or five more questions and answers, the group establishes that addictive is something that you want to keep doing. It is also established that some things addict your body and that other things addict your mind.

Next, the sheet tells Sandy to ask, "How do you stop doing an addiction?" For the next three to four minutes, based on a TV-acquired expertise, the group describes the basic steps in drug treatment: isolation from the outside world, a support group, a physical withdrawal period, admitting what is wrong, analysis and therapy, on-going support, etc.

Sandy turns the Sikhah Notes over. They say: "Step Five, Establish that *T'shuvah* is the Hebrew term for changing your life—and stopping addictive behaviors. Compare Yom Kippur to a drug treatment program." In a few more questions and answers, Sandy and the group do establish that Yom Kippur is a day to change the way you behave, especially patterns of action which are hard to break.

Then Sandy says, "I'm going to remind you of some of the elements of an addiction treatment program, and you're going to tell me how Yom Kippur does the same thing. What about isolation from the outside world."

"You spend all day in Synagogue."

"You don't eat or work or go to school."

"You spend a day away from all your normal things."

"Great," said Sandy, "What about 'a support group?'"

And so the discussion continued, establishing how Yom Kippur is like an addiction treatment program—establishing how Yom Kippur is a way of changing the way you behave.

To finish the sikhah, Sandy followed her notes and concluded with "Part Six: Evaluation, *ASK* EVERY STUDENT HOW THEY THINK THAT YOM KIPPUR WORKS." Once again, Sandy went around the circle. Just for fun, this time she went counterclockwise.

3

Night and Fog is not an easy movie to watch. It is graphic holocaust. Even the fifth or sixth time you see it, it still gets to you. It's not like a horror film where the suspense builds up to a sudden shock, or where you wait for the gore. It is calm and direct: death by business as usual. That is its real horror. The eighth grade was anxious before watching the film; they had been warned. There were a few jokes, like calling the film, "Nightmare on Stalag Street." After the film, they were docile and silent. They broke effortlessly into the three small groups. In their own way, each of the madrikhim asked two questions: "What are you feeling? What are you thinking?" The discussions started slowly, like trying to rock a car before you start to push it, then took off quickly, like the car reaching the part of the road that dips. The silence covered a real need to talk. The engine was jump started; the madrikhim actively listened.

4

Larry spread the eight cards on the table. He said, "Each card is a different way of giving tzedakah, we're supposed to put them in order from the best to the least best. Which do you think is the best way of giving?" Five or six of the hands were raised. If you looked across the room to Mrs. Klineman's group, hands went up at almost the same instant. The two groups were in deep syncromesh.

Larry called on Darbey. She grabbed the card which said, "The giver doesn't know the receiver and the receiver doesn't know the giver," and said, "I think this is the best because...

Larry cut her off, "We're not ready for explanations yet." Then he asked, "Does anyone have a different candidate for the best way to give tzedakah?"

Adam didn't wait to be called on, he grabbed the card which read "Helps him/her help him/herself." Then he said, "This one is the best one."

Larry cut him off before he could explain, saying, "Darbey and Adam, you two will be the last to speak. I want you to listen carefully to everyone else. Your job will be both to review all the arguments made for your choice as well as explain your own feelings." Then he said to the whole group, "Raise your hands if you agree with Darbey, that "Giver doesn't know receiver and receiver doesn't know giver" is the best..."

5

Class was over. Ethan walked up to Louis. He asked, "Is Yom Kippur or Rosh Ha-Shanah the holiday where we don't wear leather?"

Louis answered, "Yom Kippur is the day when lots of Jews don't wear leather."

Ethan said, "Great. I've got this radical pair of skateboarding shoes I want to wear with my Bar Mitzvah suit."

Louis said, "If your mother doesn't believe you, tell her to call me, I'll confirm that wearing your Vans is a Jewish thing to do."

Ethan smiled.

Louis said, "Peace."

Ethan said, "Later."

They slapped hands.

Chapter 6
Q & A
Classroom Communication

In this chapter we will look at the process of communication in the classroom, simply put, the way that teachers, madrikhot and students talk to each other. Our emphasis will be on conversations that teach. And, our particular focus will be the kinds of discussions which madrikhot can easily run.

Being a teacher is being a communicator. Teaching is constant dialogue; and much of it is asking questions and evoking answers from the students. As a student, you have considered and answered thousands of questions asked by dozens of teachers. As a madrikhah, you will now be asking lots of questions.

THE GOOD QUESTION

Everything in education is the subject of research. Question-asking is no exception. Research in question-asking, particularly by **P. Grossier**, reveals the obvious:.

A good question should be (1) clear, (2) purposeful, (3) brief, (4) natural and adapted to the level of the class, and (5) thought-provoking.

Even without a lot of explanation, your own experience of being a learner responding to teacher questions should inform your understanding of these five qualities.

Clear: When a question is asked, the student needs to know what is being asked. When you are asking questions, you'll discover that it is easy to ask a question which you understand but which the students don't. Usually, the problem is that part of the question is only in your mind and isn't expressed in the words you use.

An example: The teacher introduces the Mishnah, explaining that it was a collection of laws found in the Torah and expanded by the rabbis. She then explains that the Mishnah was the way that the rabbis brought the laws of the Torah up to date, they organized them in terms of the issues and problems of their own day. After this explanation, the teacher asks: "So what did the Mishnah do?"

Most of the students are ready to answer: "Collected the laws in the Torah." The teacher wanted the answer to be "Brought the laws of the Torah up to date." Can you figure out a better way to word the question to prompt the right answer?

Purposeful: A classroom is not a quiz show. Students don't receive cash prizes for correct answers. Questions in a classroom should add up to a conversation. Every question should lead a student towards an understanding (we'll talk more about this later). Questions which interrupt this flow of thinking lack a purpose.

Brief: Short is good. The simpler the question, the easier it is to understand and answer. Questions which begin with a paragraph explanation often lose or confuse students.

Use Natural and Simple Language: If students can't understand the words used in a question, they won't understand what the question is asking. Complex questions have a way of tangling themselves up so that no one can understand them. Wording questions simply is an art which takes practice.

Thought-Provoking: The best questions lead to real thinking. They ask students to do more than just recall, they enable students to achieve new understandings. When a student says, "I never thought of that before."—that is a great question.

LINES OF QUESTIONING

Because learning is a dialogue, it takes more than one question. While wording each question is important, figuring out the sequence of questions is one ultimate key to good teaching. We are going to divide this chapter into two parts. The first will talk about strategies for sequencing questions used in "frontal teaching." Frontal teaching is the kind of teaching you have probably experienced most. It is what happens when the teacher stands at the front of the room and teaches through presentation questions and activities. In the second half of the chapter, we are going to look at the art of leading discussion groups and one-on-one tutoring, the kind of teaching a madrikhah is most likely to do. In the first part we'll draw on your experience as a student to understand question asking, and in the second we'll apply it to your role as madrikhah.

BEING SOCRATES

Socrates was the Greek guy who killed himself by drinking hemlock. He was also Plato's teacher and one of the first systematic philosophers, but as far as teachers are concerned, Socrates is important because he defined an important kind of teaching conversation: The Socratic Dialogue.

A Socratic Dialogue is a way of developing theories and evolving reasoning skills. In a Socratic dialogue, a teacher poses a theory and then, through questions, forces students to examine that theory. In the end, the student either accepts or rejects the theory based on these tests.

A Sample Socratic Dialogue

T: Should a brakhah be said before or after doing an action?

S: After.

T: How do you know that?

S: Because on Shabbat we light candles first and then say the brakhah.

T: What other brakhot do we say on Erev Shabbat?

S: Kiddush and Ha-Motzi.

T: Are these said before or after the action?

S: Kiddush is before we drink the wine and Motzi is before we eat Hallah.

T: When you put on a Tallit, is the brakhah before or after?

S: After.

T: When we nail up a mezuzah, is the brakhah before or after?

S: I don't know.

T: Guess!

S: Before?

T: Right! Why did you guess before?

S: Because Tallit was before.

T: Most brakhot are said before we do the action. What is an exception?

S: Birkat Ha-mazon.

T: Right. What other exception have we found?

S: erhh..

T: Think Shabbat!

S: Oh, the Shabbat candles.

T: Why do you think that most brakhot are said before you do an action?

S: To tell you that the action is special?

T: Right, brakhot are a way of getting you ready to appreciate an experience. They get you ready for the moment. Now let's figure out why Shabbat Candles are different. What aren't you allowed to do on Shabbat?

S: Work.

T: Right. Is lighting a flame work?

S: Yes, you can't light a fire on Shabbat, that is why some Jews don't drive on Saturday.

T: Once you say the brakhah over the candles, Shabbat begins. What would happen if you said the brakhah first and then lit the candles?

S: You'd be breaking Shabbat by lighting a fire.

T: Right. So, the rabbis switched the usual order for the Shabbat candles. What do we usually do first, the brakhah or the action?

S: The brakhah.

T: Why?

S: Because it gets us ready.

T: Why are Shabbat candles an exception?

S: Because otherwise you'd light a fire on Shabbat.

T: Right.

S: Why do we say a brakhah after eating? Why is Birkat Ha-Mazon an exception?

T: That is a good question. I don't know why we say brakhot both before and after eating. I'll ask the rabbi and let you know what she says next week.

Look at this Socratic dialogue. See if you can figure out the following things:

1. What was it trying to teach?
2. What theories did the student develop?
3. How did the teacher help the student test these theories?
4. What was the **set induction**? What was the **closure**?

In order to plan a good Socratic lesson, a teacher has to be able to clearly think through the process. Good Socratic teaching takes a real focus.

BLOOMING QUESTIONS

Benjamin Bloom is a professor of educational psychology at the University of Chicago. His great contribution to the field of education is a list of levels of thinking called **Taxonomy Of Behavioral Objectives**. Simply put, **Bloom** theorizes that learning takes place in six levels: knowing, comprehending, applying, analyzing, synthesizing, and evaluating. In a little more than a paragraph we will explain each of these six levels, but first we want you to understand why they are useful. Another way to organize questions is by this taxonomy. Many educational theorists believe that a good lesson moves from the simplest thinking levels up to the most abstract.

David Ausubel is another educational theorist. One of his major contributions to the field of education was the concept of the **advance organizer**. An **advance organizer** is just what it sounds like, it is a way of organizing material in advance of learning it. For instance, in a lecture, when a teacher tells you: "Here are seven reasons why Maimonides' work changed the ways that Jews thought." You will immediately number your notebook one through seven, and have a way of grouping and remembering that material. We told you the reason **Bloom's Taxonomy** is important before we explained it, because it will help you remember and appreciate this material.

Let's climb the **Taxonomy** ladder.

1. **Knowledge** is basically facts. It is remembering or recognizing specific information. Questions beginning with **who, what, where**, and **when** are asking for knowledge.

2. **Comprehension** shows a level of understanding of information. When a student **comprehends** some material, she can organize, regroup, and/or restate it. Questions which ask a student to **give an example, compare similarities or differences, state the main idea,** or **explain in your own words** are questions which test comprehension.

3. **Application** is the level at which a student can use something she has learned to solve a problem. **Application** questions ask a student to **select the correct, use a given rule to, or classify the following**.

4. **Analysis** is a more complex form of application. In order to do an **analysis**, a student must be able to choose from among a number of possible tools and a number of possible facts. In **analysis** a student looks at something with a number of elements and explains how it works. **Analysis questions** ask a student to **identify the reason why, detect the evidence which suggests that, deduce**, or (obviously) to **analyze**.

5. **Synthesis** is sort of the opposite of analysis. In **analysis**, a student looks at the whole and breaks it into parts; in **synthesis**, she takes a number of parts and shapes them into a whole. In **analysis** a student figures out how something works, in **synthesis** a student creates her own new thing. Tasks which ask a student to **predict, create, propose, design**, etc. call for **synthesis**.

6. **Evaluation** is the ability to judge. It is the highest level of thinking because it involves all the others. In doing **evaluation** a student tests an idea or a work by using all of the lower skill levels. If you see the words **judge, decide**, or **evaluate**, you are involved in an evaluation task.

While few teachers are precise enough in their teaching to actually structure their lessons around all six levels of the **Taxonomy**, you will find that most teachers learn from experience that moving from the simple to the complicated is a successful strategy. Many lessons and many classroom dialogues will progress in a pattern similar to **Bloom's** stages.

THE *SIHAH* WAY OF LIFE

The two types of questioning strategies described above are primarily used in frontal teaching. As a madrikhah, odds are that most of your teaching will be with small groups—what in the Jewish tradition are called sihah groups.

Sihah is the Hebrew word for discussion. It is also a word with lots of Jewish educational history. Sihah is the key word in an important revolution in Jewish teaching.

Between 1890 and 1910 Jewish education went through a major revolution. (Don't worry, this is only two short paragraphs of history). Before then, the dominant form of Jewish schooling was the *Heder*. A heder was a one-room schoolhouse where a teacher called a *M'lammed* taught primarily the reading of the *Siddur* and the Bible. Students who were successful in heder got to go on to a *Yeshivah* where *Rabbis* taught the traditional sources, primarily Talmud. This was "old world" education for primarily "religious" purposes.

Starting in the late 1800's some Jews had other visions of Judaism. They wanted to learn and teach Jewish history, they wanted to write and study Jewish literature, and most of all they wanted to create a modern Jewish state. Simultaneously in Eastern Europe, Israel, and North America, these new Hebrew-centered Zionist Jews started an educational revolution. They started a whole network of modern schools where teachers who were called *Morim* taught Jewish History, Hebrew, and Literature as well as classical Jewish subjects in a modern way. And they started a whole system of Youth Movements, Summer Camps, and Youth Groups where informal education took place with older students, madrikhot, leading sihot for younger students.

Today's Jewish school is ready to renew that revolution. By becoming a good sihah leader, you can again revitalize Jewish education and help to make your classroom truly effective. In the same way that the modern State of Israel was actually created by thousands of madrikhim who taught the dream of a Jewish homeland to hundreds of thousands of their students, you too can create a dynamic Jewish future by actively listening and sharing in discussion groups. Read on, and we'll explain the power of the sihah.

In a couple of paragraphs we are going to learn about three kinds of sihot: **Teaching** sihot (Socratic and otherwise), **Task-Oriented** sihot, and **Values Reaction** sihot. Before we do that, however, we want to talk about some of the special rules for leading discussions with small groups.

ALL MY LIFE'S A CIRCLE...

Rule # 1: Sihot should be in a circle. No one should sit outside or above the circle. The sihah leader should sit at the same level as the other participants.

As in the classroom in general, the physical layout of your discussion can contribute to its success or failure. The ancient Greeks called the circle the perfect shape. In a circle, everyone is an equal member and everyone is able to see everyone else's face. That is useful to the teacher because it makes it easy to establish eye contact with everyone who is speaking and it allows you to judge from facial expressions whether or not the participants are interested in what is happening.

Another advantage of the circle is that it is easier to hear and understand someone—especially the still, small voice of a shy child—when his or her mouth is pointed towards you. In a circle, everyone speaks towards everyone else's ears. It is helpful if the diameter of the circle is kept small—it's more intimate and easier to hear if the participants sit close to each other.

The circle has at least one more advantage, in the area of classroom management. It is quite simple to reach over and put your hand on a leg or shoulder without disrupting the flow of conversation. Or, since you are facing all of the students, it is a simple matter to shoot the "evil eye" at any perpetrators of severe disorder.

Rule # 2: Always start your siḥah by formally making everyone sitting in the circle a member of the group.

In a regular class discussion there is no expectation that everyone will participate actively. Most classes are audiences. We break into small groups to give a very different sense of participation. This is part of the siḥah group's power. It is easy to detach yourself from an audience and not actively participate, when you are a member of a small group it is much harder not to be involved.

When a group is new, it is a good practice to go around the circle and make introductions. After a group knows each other (as a class does) this is silly. You should however still start a sihah with each member saying something. The act of "sharing" a feeling, or a preference, or an answer is a "ritual" of membership. It helps the people in the circle become a formal group.

After a while, even different kinds of sharing questions will grow old. After a group really knows each other, you can form the group in other ways such as (1) your saying something about each person in the group, (2) opening your comments by stating what it means to be a group, (3) or some other clever invention of your own. Lonny and Dorain, two madrikhim we know, begin every sihah by teaching their group a cheer. It is silly, but it works for them.

Rule # 3: Constantly model active listening. Never look bored or distracted (this can be accomplished with practice). Also, let your questions reflect your active listening.

Active listening is a great deal more than not making noise. You can be silent and not hear a word that is said by anyone. By active listening, we mean that each member of the sihah group is responsible for listening to what the other members are saying, trying to understand their ideas, and then sharing their own honest reactions. It is difficult to actively listen without showing that you are doing so. Look at the person who is speaking; don't lie down or play with pencils. Active listening is actually quite difficult and takes a lot of effort. Your students, once they have practiced and become proficient at it, will come to appreciate it more and more.

Two things you can do to promote active listening are asking **probe questions** and **restating**. (Yes, more **advance organizers**.)

Probe questions ask students to explain their thinking. When a student says, "I think Rosh Hashanah is the worst holiday," a good madrikhah will ask, "Why? What do you think makes it the worst?"

Restating is a way of both showing that your are listening and checking if you understand. Imagine that little Roger says, "Well, prophets were like TV news people. They got listened to. They spoke about political things and stuff. Even though they didn't have television or anything, they spoke about their opinions about what was happening and people learned from them. Some kings didn't like the prophets. Presidents don't like a lot of news guys. But, God didn't speak to Dan Rather and the prophets said, like—they were speaking for God."

At that point, you can both show Roger that you were listening (and make him feel good—another benefit of the small group) and clarify the discussion for the rest of the group by **restating**. If you say, "If I understood you correctly, you are saying, Roger, that in some ways the prophets were like TV news commentators and that in some ways they were different.

They were like TV news people in that they helped people understand political and social events. But, they were different, in that they spoke messages from God and not their own opinions."

Rule # 4: Always try to do less than 1/3rd of the talking.

This will not always be possible (especially when groups are new) or when the sihah requires that you do a lot of teaching, but you are wasting the small group format by making it into a frontal lesson in a circle. Sihot work best when they really are guided group conversations.

Rule # 5: A *sihah* should not end, it should conclude.

Don't just let someone answer the last question and then yell "break." There are lots of ways of effectively concluding a discussion and underlining its value. You can go around the circle one more time, you can summarize, you can collect "parting shots," etc., or you can even put all the hands in the center—but every sihah should reach a peak and then a specific ending.

THREE KINDS OF SIHOT

There is no formal literature on sihah group leading (perhaps someday you'll make it the topic of your doctorate in Jewish education). From our own experience, there are three basic kinds of *sihot*: **teaching sihot, task-oriented sihot,** and **values oriented/sharing sihot.** All of the basic rules mentioned above apply to each of them, but each kind also has a few unique aspects.

Teaching Si<u>h</u>ot

Teaching si<u>h</u>ot are designed to transfer information or insights. In many ways, they are traditional
"frontal lessons" done in small circles. There are many
good reasons for deciding to use a frontal lesson
rather than a large group frontal presentation:

1. Si<u>h</u>ot allow the teaching team to vary the
   instructional setting.

2. They have a much greater likelihood for motivating student involvement in the lesson.

3. Working in a small circle gives individual students hands-on practice at applying or testing a
   new skill.

4. They allow the class to be divided by ability or
   interest.

5. They give students a better opportunity to react
   to difficult or emotionally charged material.

6. They offer classroom management opportunities
   (like splitting up bad combinations).

And

7. They reflect an authentic Jewish study modality.

Reading groups (you remember them from first,
second and third grades in "real school") are a perfect
example of a teaching si<u>h</u>ah. The small group in the
circle allows the teacher to work with specific levels,
give every student a larger number of times to participate and practice, and enable some intimate conversations which would not take place with the whole
class. The same reading lesson taught to the whole
class would not work as well as three smaller reading

groups. The availability of skilled madrikhot allows teachers to switch into this kind of teaching situation.

Teaching sihot can take many forms. They can be reading groups, or do text study. They can teach Socratically or by moving questions up Bloom's levels, or in a number of other ways. Teaching sihot are lessons which take place in small groups in a circle. To make teaching sihot work takes a few basic skills:

Planning: A teaching sihah is really a lesson. It should have a beginning (a good **set induction**) a middle (it should be too short to need **stimulus variation**) and an ending (yes, a **closure**).

Active Communications: The intimacy of the circle demands the involvement of every group member. Lectures don't work in circles. The Q & A format should continually involve students in the process. Students should be copilots, helping the group reach its conclusion.

Focusing: The closeness of a small group is both exhilarating and tiring. In a regular classroom you can let your attention drift and have some privacy; in a small group, you are constantly "on-line." Groups get tired. Generally they are good ten-to-twenty-minute activities. Do only one thing in a sihah—but do it well.

Planning: (This repetition is for the sake of reinforcement). Planning is the major key to success.

Task-Oriented-*Sihot*

Often, sihah groups are one step in a lesson. In these cases, sihah groups are usually given something to accomplish: solving a problem, writing a skit, doing an art project, presenting one side of a debate, playing the part of one group in a historical simulation, etc. By breaking the class up into parallel groups, each of which works on a task, the classroom suddenly has a number of new possibilities. Groups of students led by a madrikhah who functions as a siḥah leader can accomplish wondrous things that students working alone can't come near.

Usually, in a classroom which uses group work within a lesson, the teacher does the **set-induction** with the whole class, then the groups work and report. The lesson concludes with some kind of **closure** provided by the teacher. In these cases, the role of the madrikhah is that of enabling the creative functioning of these small groups. Here are a few suggestions for this kind of group task.

Re-orient the group. Even though the teacher (or the handout) will have probably defined the group's task two or more times already, begin by going over it and defining the groups goal. You can do this by having group members state the task in their own words, or by restating it yourself. If there is a handout which gives directions, you probably want to have it read out loud, first. Your own judgment will help you decide whether you or a group member does the reading.

Three to Four Steps. When groups work on creative tasks, there are three or four basic steps: **brainstorming**, **organizing/deciding**, and then **creating**.

Brainstorming is a process of getting as many ideas as possible. The best **brainstorming** takes place when no one judges the suggestions. Group members should suggest anything that comes to mind, even if it is weird or unrealistic. Strange ideas often become workable with thought; crazy suggestions often inspire other interesting ones. A group of people can usually accomplish more by brainstorming (and "piggybacking" off each other's ideas) than the same individuals could if they were all working alone.

Organizing and Deciding are the second and third stages. Sometimes they are done at the same time, sometimes they happen separately. It depends both on the task and on the group. During **organizing**, your job is to help the group sort and order all the suggestions, to see how they fit together. For example, if the group is making a mural, **organizing** would be where the group would see how the various images would fit together. **Deciding** is where the group has to choose. There are two basic ways of deciding: **voting** and **consensus**. **Voting** is where you raise your hands and one or more sides win and others lose. **Consensus** is where a group talks and compromises and reaches a collective decision, usually taking part of all the suggestions. **Voting** is simpler and neater, **consensus** tends to be both more creative and a better group building process. There are times to do each.

Creating is where the actual work gets done. Sometimes, the work will be broken up and every individual or small teams will each do a part. Other times, the group works as a committee of the whole. The nature of the group, the kind of task, the time available, and your own preferred leadership style will all influence your choice.

Enable, Don't Dictate: The hardest part of leading a task-oriented group is deciding how much of the creativity will come from you, and how much will come from the students. Three truths:

(1) If you take over the group and do it all, students may well have a wonderful time, bringing your ideas to life—or they may resent it, and they may or may not learn from the experience.

(2) If you are just the person who decides whose turn it is to speak and leaves all the creativity and organization to the students, they may do a wonderful job, they may not do a wonderful job, and it may or may not be a wonderful learning experience.

(3) The best group creative experiences usually happen when the leader's advanced knowledge and ability can weave together and build a wonderful creation using the ideas and skills of the group. (In other words, like most other teaching skills, it's timing, judgment, and balance).

Values-Oriented *Sihot*

Sometimes, particularly when you are dealing with subjects which evoke strong emotions, there is a need just to share. Lots of feelings come bubbling to the surface, and students need to talk about them. In these cases, it is often good to break into small groups. In these kinds of situations, the si<u>h</u>ah needs to practice **active listening** skills. This is a time where the lightest touch is best.

READ MY LIPS

Overall, the effective teaching team will use good questioning skills to support and encourage class discussions. The teacher and the madrikh will have to keep several things in mind so that as many students as possible are involved in the discussion, the discussion is not simply a bull session, and the ideas lead to a deeper understanding of the content under investigation (as has already been stressed earlier in this chapter).

It is very important that the teaching team does not act as if communication means only teacher talks-students listen or teacher questions-students answer. The dynamics in the classroom are more complex than that. For education to occur, you as a member of the teaching team will want to insure that the students are actively engaged in the learning. Questions and discussions are a very critical aspect of that learning.Your role is to assist the students, not to dominate, control, or be the center of attention regarding the learning. You can help good communication happen.

CASE STUDIES

PART ONE: OBSERVATIONS

Read the following case studies. Is there a communication problem? Is there something especially nice happening? What would you do if you were the teacher in each situation? What will you do as the Madrikh in that classroom? What would you do if you were a student? After you have written down your responses, share them with the other madrikhim.

1. The fifth-grade class is discussing Sukkot. The teacher asks a factual question. Several hands go up in the air. The teacher calls on a student sitting right in front of her. As that student answers the question two students in the back say to each other, "I'm not raising my hand again, she only calls on Jim and Beth." "Yeah, she always calls on them first."

2. "That was a good answer, Rachel. I did not make the connection before between what Jon said and the story we just finished. Who else agrees with Rachel? Or is there someone who disagrees?" A student's hand goes up." I think Rachel is correct." " Okay Miriam, tell us what you agree with and why you agree?"

3. Teacher: "We have spent the last 15 minutes talking about life on a kibbutz and you have asked some good questions. Let me ask you, would you like to live on a kibbutz? Take a few minutes to

think about that. Write down your answer. When you have your answer half the class will sit with me and discuss their answers and the other half will work the same way with Rob (the Madrikh)."

4. Teacher: "Sandy, that's the stupidest answer I have ever heard from you. Don't you have your thinking cap on today? Who else wants to answer the question...not as stupidly as Sandy?"

5. Teacher: "Let's do a short brainstorm. See how many questions we can think of that would be the important kind we would want to put on a test if we were writing the test for this unit."

    Later: That is a fine list. Let's see if we can answer them and tell why we answer them the way we do.

6. Teacher: "Matt said that he thinks Bar Mitzvah is the most important life cycle event because it helps the boy have a Jewish identity. Carla, can you tell Matt why you agree or disagree with what he just said?"

PART TWO: GOOD QUESTIONS

Look at these questions. Decide which of them are good questions. Take those questions which you do *not* consider good questions and improve them by rewording them.

1. Do you think that hitting a rock was a good enough reason for keeping Moses out of the Promised Land?

2. If you were one of the Rabbis who was asked by Napoleon to be part of a modern Sanhedrin and

answer his questions, would you have participated?

3. Jessica said that the Talmud was a commentary on the Torah. What is a commentary? What does a commentary do?

4. When Jews came through Ellis Island, inspectors often changed their names. They made them shorter and easier to pronounce. They also made them sound more American. Is wiping out a heritage anti-semitism?

5. What are three names for Shavuot? What do they teach?

   (Clue: Hag Shavuot, the holiday of weeks, Hag *Bikurim*, the holiday of first fruits, and Hag *Matan Torah*, the holiday of the giving of the Torah.)

6. What started the Intifada?

7. Who can explain the name Rambam?

8. Which Jewish holiday do you think is most important? Explain your thinking.

9. The Hebrew word *gamal* means camel. The third letter in English is "C." The third letter in Hebrew is "*gimmel*." Who knows where the *gimmel* came from?

10. How many *mitzvot* are there?

PART THREE: PLANNING A SIHAH

Take one of these three teaching ideas and turn them into a sihah. Write an outline of that sihah. You may make it a Socratic discussion, a "Bloom-ladder," or some hybrid of your own, but make it good.

1. A mitzvah is not just "a good deed." A mitzvah is a "commandment," an obligation taught to the Jewish people in the Torah. When Jews accepted the Torah, they accepted the obligation to observe all the mitzvot. There are, according to tradition, 613 mitzvot. Of these 365 mitzvot, the same number as the days of the year, are positive. Positive mitzvot ask you to do something. The remaining 248 mitzvot, the number of bones in the human body, are negative mitzvot. Negative mitzvot ask you not to do something. Honoring parents is a positive mitzvah. Not stealing is a negative mitzvah. Maimonides teaches that the numbers of positive and negative mitzvot teach us to use all our human strength to always live the Torah.

2. Hannukah is really the story of a civil war, not a revolution. For the most part, the original fighting was between Jews who wanted to become more like the Greeks, and Jews who wanted to remain traditionally Jewish. Both groups tried to win support from the Syrian governor. When the arguing between these two groups got to be too much, Antiochus, the Syrian Ruler, decided that the best way to end this religious conflict was to make everyone be the same. He decided that if there were no religious differences, there would be no conflict. He ordered everyone to stop following traditional Jewish ways (like circumcision, Shabbat, and Torah study) and become Greeks. It was when

they were forced to bow to idols that the Maccabees finally organized themselves to fight back.

3. In the story of creation, it is right after creating people, that God blesses them. God gives them four blessings: (1) Be fruitful, (2) Multiply, (3) Fill the earth, and (4) Master it. People do take control, but soon the world is filled with evil. People become evil masters. Eventually, God decides that things must change. God decides to destroy all life with a flood and start over again with one, good, ethical family. After the flood God gives a three-part blessing to Noah and his family: (1) Be fruitful, (2) Multiply, and (3) Fill the earth. It is exactly the same except that "Master it" has been taken away. God no longer wants people to be in charge. Instead, God gives Noah and his family a new thing: the covenant. Now God tells people that together, God and people will master the world.

Include each of these steps in your sihah outline:

a. A way of turning those sitting in the circle into a group
b. Set induction
c. Exposition of content (Include key questions and expected answers.)
d. Closure

PART FOUR: DESIGNING A LESSON

Imagine a fifth-grade classroom with 18 students, one teacher and two madrikhot. Plan a lesson which involves the entire teaching team and which spends a portion of the time in si<u>h</u>ah groups. Choose one of these three topics.

1. The debate at the 6th World Zionist Congress over whether or not to accept Uganda as a Jewish Homeland.

2. The study of the birthright and blessing which Jacob stole from Esau.

3. The saying from Pirke Avot: "If I am not for myself, who am I? If I am only for myself, what am I? If not now, when?"

Journal Entry

Visit three classrooms in your school and observe for the following communication skills. After you have completed your observations, share your findings with the other madrikhot.

1. Count the number of questions the teacher asks during a 15-minute period of the class and time how long the teacher waits for a student to answer each question. (Obviously, you should arrange a time when there is some active teaching going on.) Keep your tally as check marks on a piece of paper.

   A. When you have completed this observation, count up the number of questions. Are you surprised by the number? Does it seem high or low? Why?

   B. Did the questions seem helpful to the learning process?

   C. How would you characterize the teacher's tone (friendly, aggressive, impatient, etc.)?

   E. Would you change anything in the way the questions were asked or phrased if you were the teacher? How?

   F. Determine average amount of time the teacher waited for the students to answer a question. Compare this "Hang time" average with that of the individual teachers. Which teachers seemed more effective—those with longer or shorter hang times? Why do you think this is?

   G. Is it possible to wait too long?

2. Count the number of questions that the students ask the teacher, the madrikhah, or each other during a 30-minute segment of the class. On a piece of paper, give each student in the class a number according to where they are sitting. You will be making a seating diagram of the class with the students all having numbers instead of names. Put a mark next to each student's number when they ask a question. The mark should be a T when the question is directed to the teacher; an M when it is to the madrikhah; an S when it is to another student.

A. Total the number of questions asked by the entire class during each observation. Compare the totals of the three teachers. Which teachers seemed more effective—those whose students ask fewer or more questions? Why do you think this is?

B. To whom are most of the questions directed during the observation? Do you think that this is important? Why or why not?

C. Did the questioning process seem to help or hinder the learning process? Why do you think so, or why not?

COMMANDMENTS FOR MADRIKHOT

NEGATIVE COMMANDMENTS

1. Do not make a practice of answering questions asked by the teacher.

2. When you are asking the questions, don't let students get away with a quick answer—pursue their line of thought. Probe for more information. "That's a good statement. Can you tell us the evidence you have found in the story to back it up?" "What steps did you go through to reach that conclusion?"

3. When leading a *sihah,* don't forget your original goals and direction. If the sihah goes off on a tangent it is important to bring it back to the subject being discussed." Let me go over what we have said so far before we continue." "We have been discussing....then David made a suggestion. Does anyone have something else to add?"

4. Don't forget that you have many students in your class. When a student finishes speaking, be sure to look around the room to see the reactions of the other students in the class. If you spot someone who looks puzzled, ask them to tell why they seem confused. If it appears that the students are agreeing with the comment and answer, you can ask them to give further evidence or examples to back up the argument.

5. Don't expect all questions to have an immediate answer. Allow time for thought before asking for responses. It is a good idea to wait at least three seconds or more for an answer.

Positive Commandments

1. Make your questions good questions. Make them clear, brief, appropriate to the level of the class, and especially—thought provoking.

2. When you run a sihah, arrange your group in some kind of circle.

3. Always start your sihah by formally involving everyone in the circle.

4. Always think through your sihah. Remember, it is a mini-lesson which needs a **set induction**, a **middle**, and a **closure**.

5. Constantly model active listening.

6. Make sure that your sihah concludes rather than just ending abruptly.

Journal Entry

This research is part of your preparation for the next unit.

1. Poll at least four adult members of the congregation and ask them to tell you what they think are some of the subjects, concepts, or ideas of Judaism one should study as an adult. Find out if any of these people have studied Judaism in some fashion since they finished their formal schooling.

2. With the help of the educator, rabbi, cantor, or other synagogue professional, make a list of programs and courses that have been offered for adult study during the past two years.

   a. Talk to a person who attended one of these programs and ask them to tell you why they enrolled. Ask them to tell you what they would like to study next.

   b. Interview a person who teaches (or taught) adults in the congregation and ask them to tell you what they teach, why they teach, and what they study for their own growth.

3. Attend a session of an adult study program or course in the congregation. As you participate pay close attention to the teaching methods the teacher uses, and how the members of the class interact with each other and the teacher.

4. Make a list of at least four things in Judaism that you would like to study (or know more about) if you had the time.

COMPULSORY JEWISH EDUCATION

A Prologue to Chapter 7

A man came to Menaḥem Mendel of Kotzk and asked how he could make his sons devote themselves to Torah.

Menaḥem Mendel answered: "If you really want them to do this, then you yourself must spend time over the Torah, and they will do as you do. Otherwise, they will not devote themselves to the Torah but will tell their sons to do it. And so it will go on."

"If you yourself forget Torah, your sons will also forget it, only urging their sons to know it, and they will forget Torah and tell their sons they should know it. And no one will ever know Torah."

Chapter 7

CONTINUING STUDY
TORAH LISHMAH

Now for the truth. Your Jewish education is not over. It is not even almost over, no matter what your parents or the synagogue rules say. Being a madrikh means that you are now starting your Jewish education for real. It means that you now have more to learn—and a good reason for learning it.

Such is the thinking of our People. The Torah is our guide to making a better world. At the same time it is synonymous with all that is Jewish learning. Torah and study are keys to the future of the Jewish community.

Aḥad Ha'Am wrote, " Learning! Learning! Learning! That is the secret of Jewish survival."

The Ḥasidim teach that a young rabbi complained to his master: "During the hours when I am studying I feel filled with light and life, but as soon as I cease to study this mood disappears. What ought I to do?"

Thereupon the master replied: "It is like a man who journeys through a forest on a dark night, and part of the way is accompanied by a companion who carries a lantern. At length they come to a point where their paths divide, and they must go on alone. If each carries his own lantern he need fear no darkness."

As a madrikh you have made a commitment to Jewish survival through study. You have made a symbolic statement that says that the world can be a better place, that the Jewish People will help bring about that better world and that, as part of the teaching team in a Jewish school, you will help educate a generation of Jews who will work with their hands, hearts and heads towards that goal of a better world. That process of education most certainly involves study. Study on the part of the students and study on your part too. The teaching team, the teachers and the madrikhim, has to also be devoted to studying on their own behalf. A learned Jew named Mauriceuels explained it this way: "For others, a knowledge of their people is a civic duty, while for the Jews it is a sacred duty."

In Jewish tradition continuing study is sometimes called *Torah Lishmah*. This is translated as study for study's sake, meaning that the purpose of this studying is to gain knowledge and wisdom, not to win an award or receive a degree. This type of study is considered a very high value. For you to be an excellent madrikh, for you to be a special role model, for you to be part of the work of the Jewish People, *Torah Lishmah* must be a high priority on your list of values. You must continue to study and learn about Judaism and what it means to be a Jew.

We are pretty sure that in order to be a madrikh you are required to be enrolled in some kind of formal Jewish education. (If not, you should be.) It is also likely that you are involved in a youth group which does some informal study. All of this is as it should be.

(If this isn't the case, you should find a regular way of continuing your Jewish education—enroll in adult education, have your rabbi set up a post-confirmation class, look into Hebrew High, etc.)

But, even if it is the case, as a madrikh you are not done. As a part of the teaching team, you should always want to have something extra to give your students. You should be reading something about each of the courses you are teaching—no matter what they are, you will always have more to learn. And, trust us, it will make a difference in the classroom. And, because you have now accepted the responsibility to be a "Jewish expert," you need to keep up on Jewish current events, etc. Yes, there is always too much to learn and know. And, yes, it is your responsibility.

"The heart of the Jewish People has always been in the Bet Hamidrash, the House of Study. There was the source from which they drew the strength and inspiration that enabled them to overcome all difficulties and withstand all persecutions. If we want to go on living, we must restore the center to the Bet Hamidrash, *and make that once more the living source of Judaism."* (Aḥad Ha'Am)

PRACTICUM

This is a hard, confusing, complex but very interesting piece of Talmud. It comes from *Bava Batra*, the last of three books which center on "damages," and in the middle of talking about the rights of neighbors, it begins to talk about Jewish teaching. It will take a couple of tries to work through, but when you've finished you will (1) understand something about how Talmud thinks, and (2) have done some interesting thinking on your own about the real nature of Jewish teaching.

It should make for a good *Torah Lishmah* experience.

Bava Batra 20b-22a

MISHNAH

IF A PERSON WANTS TO OPEN A SHOP IN A COURTYARD,
THE NEIGHBORS MAY PREVENT THE SHOP ON THE GROUNDS

THE NOISE OF THE PEOPLE COMING AND GOING
MAY KEEP THEM FROM SLEEPING.

A PERSON, HOWEVER, MAY MAKE ARTICLES IN THE COURTYARD
AND THEN TAKE THEM OUT AND SELL THEM IN THE MARKET.
THE NEIGHBORS MAY NOT PREVENT THIS ON THE GROUNDS
THAT:
THE NOISE OF THE HAMMER,
THE NOISE OF THE MILLSTONES,
OR THE NOISE OF CHILDREN
KEEPS THEM FROM SLEEPING.

BARTINORA: THE NOISE OF CHILDREN REFERS TO THE
NOISE MADE BY THE CHILDREN WHO COME
TO PATRONIZE THE SHOPS.

GEMORA

Cast:

Abaye
Rabba
Rav
The Voice of the Torah
Joshua Ben Gamala
Narrator
The voice of the Baraita
Rashi
Tosefot
Rabbi Gershom
Rabbi Dimi from Nehardea
King David
Joab
Joab's Teacher

Part One: The Basic Debate

Narrator 1:   *The rabbis began their discussion of
this Mishnah by asking:* Why is the
rule in the second case, *which says
that neighbors can't complain about
the noise of children visiting shops,* different from the rule in the first case,
*where neighbors can complain about
other customers?*

Abaye:	The second part must refer to *a person manufacturing in* another courtyard.
Rabba:	*Abaye*, If *you were* right, the Mishnah would say, In another courtyard it is permissible. Therefore, *Abaye*, You are wrong.
	The second part of this Mishnah is talking about the noise made by school children *studying*.

1. Abaye and Rabba are arguing over the meaning of "children" in the Mishnah. Explain the difference in interpretation.

2. Why do the rabbis work hard to keep "the noise of children" from meaning the obvious?

Part Two: An Aside about Joshua Ben Gamala

	Rabbi Judah taught us that Rav taught him:
Rav:	The name of the man who is to be blessed is Joshua ben Gamala, were it not for him, the Jewish people would have lost the Torah. In the beginning, every son was taught by his father—and if he had no father, he did not learn.
Narrator:	They learned this practice from Deuteronomy 11.19:
Torah:	AND YOU SHALL TEACH THEM TO YOUR CHILDREN...
Narrtor:	This practice emphasized the word:
Torah:	YOUR.

Rav: Then they made it an ordinance that teachers of young children should be appointed in Jerusalem.

Rabba: They evolved this practice from the prophet Isaiah 2.3:

Isaiah: FROM ZION SHALL GO FORTH THE LAW AND THE WORD OF THE LORD FROM JERUSALEM.

Rav: Even so, after this practice began, if a child had a father, the father would take him up to Jerusalem and have him taught there, and if he did not have a father, he would not go up and learn. They therefore ordained that teachers should be appointed in each Roman administrative district (Prefecture), and that boys should enter school at the age of sixteen or seventeen. It came to pass that when teachers tried to discipline students of this age, the students would rebel and then leave school.

Finally, Joshua ben Gamala came and ordained:

Joshua B G: Teachers of young children should be appointed in each district and each town. Children should enter school at the age of six or seven.

1. Explain how each of the biblical verses influenced the way Jewish schools were first established.

2. What does this history teach us about the relationship of the Jewish school and the Jewish home?

3. What else is interesting here?

Part Three: Selected Thoughts about Jewish Teaching

Narrator:	Rav said to Rabbi Samuel ben Shilat:

Rav: Do not accept students below the age of six. You can accept them after that age and stuff them with Torah like an ox.

Narrator: Rav also said to Rabbi Samuel ben Shilat:

Rav: When you punish a child, only hit him with a shoe lace. An attentive child will motivate himself. Place an inattentive child next to a diligent one.

1. There are four pedagogic hints given here. Explain and evaluate each one.

2. If you were Rav, what hints about Jewish teaching would you give Rabbi Shilat?

Part Four: A Return to the Debate

Narrator: *Now we return to our original question about the Mishnah. How can the same Mishnah suggest that the noise made by adult customers can prevent a business from being opened in a courtyard, but the noise made by children can't?*

*One of the rabbis, who is not named, disagrees with Rabba's explanation that the noise of children refers to noise of children in school which should be permitted. He quotes a **baraita**, (an older legal decision of the same age as the Mishnah, but not included in it).*

Baraita 1:	If the resident of a courtyard wishes to open a business as a *mohel*, a blood-letter, a tanner, or a teacher of children *in his house*, the other residents can prevent him.
Rabba:	This refers to a teacher of non-Jewish children.
Narrator:	*Then the rabbi who is arguing with Rabba quotes a second baraita.*
Baraita 2:	Come and learn. If two people live in a courtyard and one of them wishes to open a business as a *mohel*, a blood-letter, a tanner, or a teacher of children, the other can prevent him!
Rabba:	This, too, refers to a teacher of non-Jewish children.
Narrator:	*Then the rabbi who is arguing with Rabba quotes a third baraita.*
Baraita 3:	Come and learn. If a person has a room in a public courtyard, he must not rent it to a *mohel*, a blood-letter, a tanner, a *sofer*, or a non-Jewish teacher.

1. Explain the differences between the three *baraitot*.

2. The key to third *baraita* is the addition of the word *sofer*. Look below and explain how it changes the nature of the argument.

Part Five: Four Comments on One Word

Rashi:	Where *sofer* usually means scribe, here it refers to a Jewish teacher.

Tosafot:	Here, the word *sofer* means a town scribe who would have a large number of visitors coming to him.
R. Gershom	Here, the word is actually *sapar*, a barber, not a *sofer. (The text has no vowels).*
Rabba:	This refers to the head teacher of a town, *the own who supervises all the others.*

1. Again, the rabbis work hard to keep "the noise of children" from meaning the obvious. Why are neighborhood Jewish schools so important to them?

2. Is their interpretation "fair?"

Part Six: Additional Thoughts About Jewish Teaching

Narrator:	*Rabba also taught five other things about education. First:*
Rabba:	According to the ruling of Joshua ben Gamala, children should not be regularly made to attend school in another town, but they can be made to attend school in another synagogue in the same town. However, if the other synagogue is across a river, we cannot make them attend. But, if there is a bridge across the river, we can make them attend. But, if the bridge is only a plank, we cannot make them attend.
Narrator:	*Second:*

Rabba:	The maximum number of students who are to be assigned to each teacher is twenty-five. If there are fifty, we appoint two teachers. If there are forty, we appoint an assistant, at the expense of the town.
Narrator:	*Third:*
Rabba:	If there is a teacher who has some relationship with his students and there is a second teacher who has much better relationships with students, we do not replace the first with the second, because without competition the second may grow lazy.
R.Dimi	You do appoint the new teacher because he would exert himself even more, because the jealousy of teachers increases wisdom.
Narrator:	*Fourth:*
Rabba:	If there are two teachers and one teaches quickly but with mistakes and the other teaches slowly but without mistakes, we appoint the fast teacher who makes mistakes, because mistakes correct themselves in time.

1. Do you agree with R. Dimini or Rabba? Why?

2. How would you characterize a great Jewish teacher?

3. Find the only mention of madrikhim in the Talmud.

Part Seven: The Story of Joab's Teacher

R. Dimi: We appoint the one who teaches more slowly but without mistakes. We learn this in the Bible, 1 Kings 11.16:

Torah: FOR JOAB AND ALL ISRAEL REMAINED THERE UNTIL HE HAD CUT OFF EVERY MALE IN EDOM.

R. Dimi: When Joab came before King David, David said to him:

David: Why did you only kill the male Edomites?

Joab: Because it is written in Deuteronomy 25.19: "TORAH: YOU SHALL BLOT OUT KOL Z'KHAR AMALEK, ALL THE MEN OF AMALEK."

David: But the Torah says:

Torah: "YOU SHALL BLOT OUT KOL ZEKHER AMALEK, ALL THE MEMORY OF AMALEK."

Joab: I was taught that the word was Z'KHAR.

R. Dimi: Joab then went and saw his teacher. He asked him:

Joab: How did you teach me to read this verse?

Teacher: Z'KHAR.

R. Dimi: Then, Joab took our his sword and threatened to kill his teacher.

Teacher: Why do you do this?

Joab: Because it is written in Jeremiah 47.10:

Torah:	CURSED BE HE THAT DOES THE WORK OF THE LORD NEGLIGENTLY.
Teacher:	Don't kill me. Be satisfied that I am cursed.
Joab:	It also says in that verse:
Torah:	CURSED BE HE THAT KEEPS HIS SWORD BACK FROM BLOOD.
R. Dimi:	One report says he did kill him. Another report says he didn't.

1. Explain this story in your own words? What is the problem? What is the message?

2. Can you give your own example of a teacher whose teaching is dangerous?

3. What do you think Joab did?

Part Eight: A Final Thought About Jewish Teaching

Narrator:	This is Rabba's fifth lesson about Jewish teaching:
Rabba:	A teacher of young children , a vine-keeper, a *shoḥet*, a blood-letter, and a *sofer* are all liable to immediate dismissal. The general principle is that anyone whose mistakes cannot be corrected, is liable to immediate dismissal if a mistake is made.

1.Explain this ruling in your own words.

2. How does knowing that you are liable to immediate dismissal influence your work?

Journal Entry

Interview at least three teachers in your school. Ask them:

1. How did they come to be Jewish teachers?
2. What else do they do? Is this the way they earn their living?
3. Why do they do this?
4. What do they get out of it?

YOUR BLESSING

A Prologue to Chapter 8

Rabbi Levi taught in the name of Rabbi Joḥanan:

"A man set out on a journey and traveled a day, two days, three days, up to ten days, without finding either a town, a wayside inn, a tree, water, or any living thing. After having traveled ten days—when he was about to give up hope—he spied a tree in the distance and thought,'There may be water beneath it.'

When he came near, he found that indeed it stood by a fountain. Seeing how beautiful the boughs of the tree were, he sat down to cool himself in the shade. Then he ate of the fruit of the tree, drank the water, and felt pleased and refreshed.

When he rose up he said, addressing the tree, 'What blessing can I bestow upon you or what parting word can I offer you? That your wood be fine? It is fine. That your shade be pleasant? It is pleasant already. That your boughs be fair? They are fair. That your fruit shall be luscious? Luscious it is already. That a fountain shall flow beneath your roots? It does already. That you shall stand in a desirable spot? Why, you do stand in a desirable spot. What blessing can I give you? Only that all your saplings that shall spring from you shall be just like you.'"

You are that tree. You, as a madrikhah, are growing tall and strong. You will spread the branches of your Jewish knowledge and love of the Jewish People over all the students with whom you work.

Chapter 8
A Madrikhah: Your Work and Your Future

In the prologue to this book, Joel Grishaver introduced you to the curse of Joshua Mereminsky, "May your students do to you only half of what you've done to your teachers." By now you should realize that this curse is really a blessing, because it comes with a laugh. When Balaam went to curse the Jewish people, God transformed the curse into a blessing. His curse came out as the prayer we now use to enter the synagogue: *Ma Tovu.*

This year, though you may never admit it to your parents, teachers, or friends, the bitterness which may have often surrounded your Jewish education has been washed away. Not every moment of it was perfect. And, clearly, you sacrificed for it, missing many things you really wanted to do. But now, this year, through seeing the other side, its real purpose should come through.

Jewish teaching is really a privilege and a reward. We know a Jewish teacher whose children ask him where he is going every time he leaves for work. Every day, his answer is the same, "I am going to save the Jewish world." As a madrikhah you have a tremendous responsibility. You are working with the future leaders and members of the Jewish community. You are responsible for making sure that the next generation of Jews is educated, dedicated and committed.

Every year when I work with my students at the Hebrew Union College, I make an interesting discovery. Each year, when we talk about why they decided to choose to become rabbis, cantors, or Jewish educators, I expect that they will each talk about some teacher, rabbi, or cantor they have had. I expect that they will say they want to grow up to be like them. But, that is almost never the case. Instead, they tell a different story. Usually it has been the experience of being a teacher, being a youth leader, or being a camp counselor that has made the difference. They chose to work in Jewish education because the work itself is rewarding; it was the nature of their first work experiences which drew them to want more. We suspect that it may well happen to you, too.

It is almost certain that you will become a Jewish teacher. For, if nothing else, it is highly likely that you will become a Jewish parent. (Our friend, Jerry Kaye, regularly teaches his madrikhim that "the future of Judaism is in your pants.") When you become a Jewish parent, you will be your child's first Jewish teacher.

But, there are other Jewish teaching positions to consider. There are many Jewish ways to earn a living. Jewish professions include synagogue work (Rabbis, Cantors, Educators, Administrators, etc.), communal service (Centers, Federations, Agencies), informal education (Camps, Family Education, Youth Groups), academia (Jewish professors and professors of Judaica), and lots more.

And, just because you may choose to earn your living in other ways, that doesn't mean that Jewish teaching isn't in your future. Probably half the Jewish teachers in North America do other things for a living and teach in Jewish schools out of love and commitment. Plus, even if you never return to work in a classroom after being a madrikhah, there are other lay roles which are important. Being a synagogue leader, a federation board member, a chairman of the education committee, etc. are all important ways of enabling Jewish learning.

You also have your own future to consider. The Jewish community needs you. There is a great need in the Jewish community today for the kind of commitment you have demonstrated by your work as a madrikhah. The Jewish People need you and your fellow madrikhim to stay very involved in the Jewish community.

Your work as a madrikhah is a giant step in the right direction. The experience that you get as a madrikhah will be invaluable to you as a Jewish teacher or educator. By the time you have finished your tenure as a madrikhah, you will be on your way towards being a Jewish teacher. You have the opportunity to offer a great contribution to the Jewish People and at the same time dedicate your life to a most fulfilling task...educating the next generation.

If any of this sounds interesting, there are a few things we want you to consider:

1. Get yourself to Israel. Make your parents send you on a high school program or during one of your years of college.

2. Work at a Jewish summer camp (day or sleep over).

3. When you get to college, take some Jewish course-work, and join Hillel, or some other Jewish campus group.

4. Get yourself to a CAJE conference (The Conference on Alternatives in Jewish Education.) This is an annual gathering of close to 2,000 Jewish teachers. CAJE has special programs and scholarships for both high school and college students.

5. Talk to your rabbi, camp director, youth advisor, or educator about your Jewish future.

Trust us; each of these things can change your life.

As you grow older, you will have those saplings—those former students—who will come back to see you. You will have these saplings working with you as part of a teaching team. But this time you will be the teacher and they will be the madrikhot. Remember, it is now your responsibility to curse the next generation into becoming Jewish teachers.

AN OPEN LETTER TO TEACHERS, EDUCATORS, AND DIRECTORS OF MADRIKHIM PROGRAMS

Joel Lurie Grishaver

*L*et's start with the conclusion: Creating a successful madrikhim program means changing the way your school functions. You will be making these changes, not only because it will make for a better experience for your madrikhim, but because it will enable your madrikhim to create much better experiences for your entire school. In the course of this epilogue we will be making the following recommendations:

1. That madrikhim be deployed in groups of two to three madrikhim in specially chosen classrooms rather than in the traditional one-madrikh-per-teacher pattern.

2. That teachers who work with madrikhim be trained in the process as well as the madrikhim. *If they don't attend special sessions, they should at least receive copies of this book.*

3. That madrikhim programs focus on tenth to twelfth grade students. Where younger students are involved, the intellectual and emotional standards should be set by older students.

4. That where eighth-graders are invited to join madrikhim programs they should be brought

along slowly. Their first experiences should be a series of observations of various classrooms and learning about the school. Where possible, a whole year should function as an "M.I.T" (Madrikhim In Training) program.

5. That madrikim training should focus more on "counseling" and less on "teaching" skills. The primary roles for which a madrikh should be trained are (1) coverage in large and small group settings, (2) active participation in group activities, (3) tutoring, and (4) sihah leading.

6. That every madrikh should receive an exit interview which tracks him towards Jewish experiences in college and towards future experiences in Jewish education.

7. That every madrikh be encouraged to become a teen member of CAJE (there is a special $ 10.00 membership fee) and thereby become part of the international community of Jewish teachers.

Reflections on Practice

When Sam started working on **The Madrikhim Handbook**, we assumed that the task would be fairly simple. It was to be a basic research process, a *Tze u'Lomed*, a look-and-see. Our initial plan was simply to collect the best of what is already being done. What we quickly discovered was, that while there are a few successful madrikhim programs and a lot of almost adequate ones, there is really little understanding of either the nature or the potential of having high school students (and perhaps oldish junior high school students) working in Jewish schools.

Little had changed from my own teen experiences working in Jewish schools and from my own first attempts at involving a madrikh. In the prologue, I spoke of my own transformation from school terror to office aide. In 1966, I could not become a madrikh. The term was unknown; the concept was also unknown. Teachers in my Religious school were certified Jewish teachers; college graduates with a special certificate. There were no teaching assistants. I was an office aide. I was specifically hired to collect and count *Keren Ami*, run errands, and perform that significant Jewish communal task: collating. My teaching experiences were carefully limited to Hebrew Tutoring (for which I received an extra wage—it was a different job) and occasionally filling in in a classroom until a real substitute could be found. At sixteen I was frustrated by being locked out of the classroom, so with everyone's help and approval, I started going to the Academy of Jewish Studies, earning graduate units towards my teaching certificate. That world is long gone. There is no more Academy of Jewish Studies. There aren't, in most places, functional standards for who can teach. And, in almost no school would an active, involved, teenager be officially limited to counting *Keren Ami*. Yet, similar tasks still make up the majority of most madrikim experiences.

My first madrikh was Mike. His face is still there, but his last name is long forgotten. I was a graduate student earning rent money by teaching at Leo Baeck Temple. He was a junior and then a senior in high school, a kid who had grown up at Leo Baeck. Our students were seventh- to ninth-graders, the kings of the Sunday morning hill. Mike and I talked a lot. He even came over for dinner once or twice each year. We went out to lunch a couple of times after class, too. During class, Mike took attendance, helped kids with seat work, occasionally led a small group, but mostly sat in the back and listened. He seemed to enjoy it. But I never really knew what to do with him. He didn't really have the skill or background to "teach" that class, and I was far too busy to rethink my teaching (or often even pre-think my teaching) to actively include him. Because we were with an older class, Mike was spared the indignities of juice and cookies.

When I think of Mike, I also think of Steven, another Leo Baeck student who did three years of classes with me. My last year there, he was in ninth grade. Leo Baeck starts madrikhim in confirmation, tenth grade. The first day of school, Steven came and told me that next year he wanted to be my madrikh. I was really honored and confused. I knew he was serious, and that this was a real compliment, but I never understood why he wanted the chance to sit in the back of my room and listen for a third year. Before his time came, I got my degree and took another job. Often, since then, I've wondered how I would have given Steven a better growth experience than the one I provided Mike. In certain ways, consulting with Sam on the development of this material has fulfilled those unresolved questions.

As I worked with Sam on this book, Mike and Steven came to mind often. It became clear that this book couldn't be a book about what is; rather, it had to be a book about what could, and in fact probably should be. We know that at present most teachers aren't equipped to handle madrikhim effectively, that most schools haven't addressed the questions about what a madrikh should be, and that as yet there is neither a secular nor a Jewish literature about the madrikhim experience. Therefore, we have had to do a lot of reflecting as we attempt to influence practice.

WHY WE HAVE MADRIKHIM

Synagogues create madrikhim programs for a number of reasons, though these reasons are not of equal weight.

1. It is important to have older students around the school. In this day and age, it is easier to give them a job than keep them engaged in studying (more than one night a week.)

2. Madrikhim serve as important role models.

3. Madrikhim can relieve teachers, particularly the teachers of younger children, of many of their administrative responsibilities.

4. Madrikhim can enable certain kinds of instruction.

In our experience reason number four is the most verbalized while reason number one is the most practiced. In fact, Jewish schools should have no embarrassment about reason number one, affirming that madrikhim programs are more for the benefit of the madrikhim than for the classes in which they work. In fact, publically affirming this, gives us a sense of clear direction. In biblical times, at least from what the

Bible tells us, Jewish leaders practiced on sheep. The way to learn to lead the Jewish people was by entering a shepherd-in-training program. Moses, Aaron, Saul and David are a few of the successful graduates of such programs. When both Camp Ramah and the Union Institutes were created, their respective ideologues had no embarrassment about stating that one of the major purposes of these camps was to employ and train a generation of Jewish counselors who would become the future leaders of other Jewish programs. *Mador*, *Machon* and other C.I.T. programs really did create the next generation of North American Jewish leaders, us. In the past fifteen years, the model has been extended to the Jewish school. It is clearly our hope that the next generation of American Jewish leadership will grow through madrikhim programs.

Experience suggests that successful madrikhim programs offer four elements: _hevraschaft_, bonding/mentoring with/from Jewish educational leaders, opportunities for significant learning, and rewarding work experiences. The last of these, rewarding work experiences, is clearly the most significant, and the ultimate determiner of the value and interaction of the other factors.

In truth, (and Mike and Steven would testify if we could find them) it isn't easy to involve a madrikh in a classroom, especially an older or content-driven classroom. It takes careful planning, coordination, and communication. But it can be done effectively, and it can change the nature of instruction.

THE JOB OF BEING A MADRIKH

Until recently, most madrikhim were called "teacher aides." It was an unfortunate choice of language, not only because of its homonymic relationship to AIDS, but because it is a bad model. We get much further if we think of madrikhim as analogous to "junior counselors" than we do if we classify them as "assistants-to-teachers." Consider the difference:

Teacher Aides are sort of classroom scrub nurses whose job it is to relieve the teacher of the dirty work, thereby allowing the teacher to focus more quality time on the students. Meanwhile, these junior teachers-in-training wait for the day when the teacher is out sick, or when they are kindly granted a few moments for trial teaching. Because of their age, their previous roles as "scrub nurses," their lack of Jewish content knowledge, and their lack of experience—these trial runs are usually failures.

Junior Counselors are focused on relating to kids. They start out as "active-co-participants" in experiences and move toward small group leadership. They are given constantly significant roles and can be granted an escalating series of responsibilities. They can move from success to success.

Once the new metaphor is accepted, it automatically changes the deployment, training, and supervision of madrikhim.

Our reflection and our research (particularly into camp models) suggests two deployments of madrikhim other than the usual "one-teacher, one-mad-rikh" model. While some teachers are brilliant exceptions who prove this rule through their unique skill, most madrikhim in those settings will end up like Mike, taking roll and listening.

A MADRIKH-CENTERED CLASSROOM

In the ordinary religious school classroom, a teacher has a choice of three kinds of activities: frontal teaching, seat work, and unsupervised group work. In a classroom with madrikhim, supervised group work allows for many interesting new possibilities: learning centers where each center has a facilitator, complex creative tasks where each group has an "adult" leader, reading groups which can meet simultaneously, simulation games where complex positions can be re-explained and enacted, etc.

It is unrealistic to expect most sixteen-year-olds to teach a class of twelve to twenty students. It is equally unrealistic to expect most of them to succeed at leading a group made up of half the class while the teacher works with the other half. The situation however, changes if two madrikhim each work with a half while the teacher provides floating supervision. In this latter case, (1) the madrikh is no longer in competition with the teacher, (2) the task can be structured for the ability and background of the madrikhim, and (3) the teacher is still available as a resource and source of authority.

In a classroom structured for the use of madrikhim, the teacher has the ability to constantly go back and forth between whole-class activities, which she runs, and small-group tasks, which the madrikhim handle. Consider the following difference:

Option 1: The teacher sends a group of five rambunctious eleven-year-olds into the library to create and then present a five-minute play of the book of Jonah. The teacher is able to provide the group with six sentences worth of directions (stated twice) and a copy of the book of Jonah.

Option 2: Dorian, a rambunctious seventeen-year-old (a third-year madrikh who goes to Hebrew High) takes five rambunctious eleven-year-olds into the library to create and present a five-minute play of the book of Jonah.

Answer the following:

1. Which group is more likely to create a discipline problem?
2. Which group is more likely to read and understand Jonah?
3. Which group is more likely to have a positive learning experience?
4. Which group is more likely to produce a quality experience for the rest of the class?

In a classroom structured around the use of multiple madrikhim, quality group work can regularly take place. On purpose, the above model only involves one madrikh. We assume that Mrs. Alper is busy teaching some other lesson to the rest of the class and that this is a special experience. In a multiple-madrikh-centered room, while Dorian is busy doing Jonah, Loni is working with another group on the book of Ruth, and Esti is creating a musical version of Kohelet. Meanwhile, Mrs. Alper is making the rounds. In such a class, the madrikhim are constantly challenged, and the teacher has a wonderful repertoire of activities not possible—at least, not at the same level of quality, in other classrooms.

A caveat: Not all teachers are good at sharing and supervising. This kind of deployment model lets you focus the madrikhim experience on those teachers from whom it will be successful as well.

THE TRAINING OF MADRIKHIM:

The goal of a madrikhim program is to create future Jewish leaders. In that sense, it is designed as a transition between being a Jewish student and going to college. A program that only involves eighth and ninth graders and has nothing left for older students fails to achieve that goal. Therefore, a program for madrikhim should have growth built into it. Each year should represent new challenges. We recommend a three-tiered process.

By and large, eighth- and even many ninth-graders do not have the secular education background, Jewish background, or life experience to serve in active leadership roles. That doesn't mean that they can't be valuable or have a valuable experience. Conventional wisdom says that a madrikhim program for junior high school students should be one or both of two kinds of things. One kind is a training program which centers on classroom observations and learning, rather than on doing. A second kind of program places them in classroom helping roles in the youngest grades. As a *starting* role, being a classroom helper—especially in younger grades—is a worthwhile experience. It lets madrikhim learn and practice one-on-one teaching and coverage issues, while you build other skills. A year of observations of classrooms all over the school and collective reflection will also build a sense of professionalism which you will exploit later in their training.

Tenth- and eleventh-graders are ready for the kind of "junior counselor" experience we have favored previously. It is for them that the majority of the core curriculum of this **Madrikhim Handbook** was created. We have chosen to center their training on the following skills:

a. A profound sense of the culture and traditions of your school.

b. An active sense of good coverage. They should know where to place themselves in any situation and how to control and influence the group through covert action.

c. The ability to perceive student needs and temperaments. When they look at a group of students, they should have a sense of the individuals and their needs, and also of the group.

d. The diverse skills of leading small groups both in formal discussions and in the active creation of projects.

As secondary goals, we want to expose them to some aspects of the esoteric knowledge of the teaching profession. These are things we want them to know about, but do not expect them to master:

e. Basic theories of child development

f. The basic strategies and patterns of lesson planning

g. Theories and styles of classroom management.

This secondary list allows them to (1) appreciate the work of their master teacher, (2) enter into dialogue with other members of the educational team, and (3) have some sense of the richness of insight which awaits them if they choose to enter Jewish education as a profession or avocation.

The end goal of being a madrikh, the high point which makes it all worthwhile, should be "grouping" not soloing. If we were training teachers, then that solo moment of taking over the class would be the high point (and it will come later in their lives if they do go on to a teacher training program). In our reflection, we turn again to the summer camp, where the madrikhim usually "have their moment" by planning and running a special program for the whole camp. It is our sense that the execution of one or more all-school (or all-department, etc.) programs is the right kind of culmination for twelfth grade madrikhim. In this way, working with their advisor/trainer (or the school's educational leadership), and utilizing their younger madrikhim as active-co-participants, the madrikhim are given a final challenge which both puts them directly in the spotlight (modeling the program) and which benefits the school through their creativity and energy. It is, most importantly, an event whose success can be assured both by its nature and by the active involvement of their advisor.

THE CROSS-TRAINING OF MADRIKHIM

We know from experience that Jewish content is one major key to ensuring the success of madrikhim and future Jewish teachers. Many of the madrikhim we have seen in the classroom just don't know enough about the Judaic content to be successful. They have acquired the group skills, the teacher tricks, and the interpersonal presence—they know how to teach, they just don't have the what.

The more Jewish content we can give to them, the greater their shot at success. More importantly, the more they come to value their own Jewish learning, the more likely they are to make a long-term commitment to an active role in Jewish life. It is generally the practice of most schools to insist that in order to be madrikhim, students must also be enrolled in some kind of formal Jewish education on their own. This is all well and good, but it is not enough. We therefore make two recommendations which transcend present practice.

First, madrikhim should do some crash learning about the course(s) being taught in the classes where they work. Making them read one or two adult books (not kids' textbooks) about the subject (at least the key subject) is both a good model and a good practice.

It also forms the basis of a good tutorial between them and their master teachers. (More of this later).

Second, madrikhim ought to have access to some elite Jewish learning experiences which are intentionally optional. These can be a special class, four evenings at the home of the rabbi or the educator, or a weekend with a special guest scholar, etc. But some serious learning should be part of the model.

MADRIKHIM TRAINING AS TEACHER TRAINING

Part of this model suggests that every teacher who works with a madrikh is a well-trained master teacher. We know that this is no longer a good assumption. Many will be, but many will be well-meaning and naturally talented avocational teachers. We believe that the madrikhim program provides schools with opportunities for new kinds of in-service models and new kinds of instructional models. Just as we have learned through family education experiments that it is possible to teach parents and kids together, and to motivate parents to do learning (they've been meaning to do and haven't gotten around to) so that they can teach their own kids, the same analogy should be true of madrikhim and teachers, especially teachers who make an active choice to work with madrikhim.

We suggest that this teacher training take place on two levels. First, that teachers should receive a couple of hours of instruction on how to plan to involve madrikhim. These sessions should focus on small group programming models, looking at the balance of frontal teaching, seat work, and diverse group activities.

Secondly, the teacher can also train the madrikhim in one of four ways.

Option 1: The teachers working with the madrikhim can form a training team which works through the madrikhim course with them. Like parents, they may be learning or relearning some elements of formal education before reteaching them to their students.

Option 2: The teachers working with madrikhim can serve as pedagogic tutors, working through this handbook in a series of individual meetings with their students. This can enact real mentoring.

Option 3: Teachers can join madrikhim for some or all of their training sessions. Some portion of each of these training sessions can follow the course of study included here, while other portions should actively center on team building.

Option 4: Teachers can be given their own copies of the madrikhim handbook and be asked to complete it on their own time, as a way of coordinating what the madrikhim are learning with their classroom experiences. Even in this fourth model, one or two "staff who work with madrikhim" meetings will be helpful.

YOUR REWARDS

Schools with weak madrikhim programs ultimately undercut the value of the program. Where no older students remain as madrikhim, the pediatric nature of Jewish schooling is heavily underlined. Where madrikhim are not actively involved, they tend to reduce the seriousness of the learning process. (You all know—where they hang out together when they should be in class as do eighty percent of the kids over ten in your school.)

Schools which actualize this kind of dynamic madrikhim program are in for three rewards. First, your school is filled with active role models of what it means to grow up successfully in your congregation. Second, you have a school with a flexible instructional base and an ability to get close to each student. And finally, you will be developing a Jewish leadership base which will guarantee the future of the Jewish people and perhaps the redemption of the cosmos.

P.S.

If you are a madrikh or madrikhah who just made it through this essay, congratulations. Now, nothing will be done behind your back.